Puerto Rico's Revolt for Independence

EL GRITO DE LARES

To my father Santos Jiménez,

who defied tradition and

sent me to school

Puerto Rico's Revolt for Independence
EL GRITO DE LARES

Olga Jiménez de Wagenheim

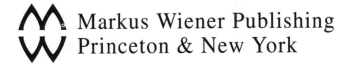

Markus Wiener Publishing
Princeton & New York

For information write to: Markus Wiener Publishing, Inc.
114 Jefferson Road, Princeton, NJ 08540

Library of Congress Cataloging-in-Publication Data

Wagenheim, Olga Jiménez de.
        Puerto Rico's revolt for independence: el Grito de Lares/
    Olga Jiménez de Wagenheim.
        Originally published in 1985
        Includes bibliographical references.
        ISBN 1-55876-071-7 (pbk.)
        1. Puerto Rico—History—Insurrection, 1868.   2. Puerto
    Rico—Economic conditions.   3. Puerto Rico—Social conditions.
    I. Title
    F1973.W34 1993   93-15391
    972.95'04—dc20   CIP

Printed in the United States of America on acid-free paper

Contents

Tables

Preface

The Spanish edition of this book, *El Grito de Lares: sus causas y sus hombres* first appeared in Puerto Rico under the imprint of Ediciones Huracan (1984). It was extensively reviewed by scholars, history buffs, and journalists in the local press, as well as in some academic journals. It was rewarding to see that they found the book to be a balanced study of a very important, and highly emotional, event.

Shortly after it appeared in print, it was adopted for classroom use in courses of Puerto Rican history offered by the major universities and colleges throughout the island. The continuous interest in the book has recently led Ediciones Huracan to come out with a third edition.

Interest in the book by scholars and students in the field of Puerto Rican studies in the United States has led to the present edition in English that is affordable for college students.

My interest in the Puerto Rican uprising, known as El Grito de Lares, was first awakened when I was an undergraduate student at the University of Puerto Rico. Although I had no idea at the time that I would one day write a book on the subject, I knew then that I was not satisfied with the accounts provided by the materials I was reading. But as often happens, other interests claimed my attention until years later.

Having by then co-edited a book of documents on Puerto Rico's history, I was aware that much of the official documentary evidence surrounding El Grito de Lares was for the first time available in Puerto Rico. From 1898 to the mid-1970s, the bulk of the island's documents regarding its colonial period under Spain had been laying unclassified in the basement of the Library of Congress. But the persistence of the late historian Dr. Arturo Morales Carrion had changed that, and the documents had not only been returned to the Puerto Rican government, but were accessible to researchers in the archive of San Juan.

An extensive review of the secondary literature, and more mature considerations of the subject. led me to formulate a research plan that would enable me to answer some of the unanswered questions, as well as to correct many of the flagrant contradictions about "the facts" that permeated the available writings about the Lares Uprising and its players. This book is the product of that search.

As with any book of this scope, the present study could not have been carried out without the pioneering work of others. To the historians Salvador Brau, Lidio Cruz Monclova, Loida Figueroa, Labor Gomez Acevedo, and Arturo Morales Carrion, among others, I will always be indebted for their valuable roles in bringing to light the importance of the Lares Uprising. I also extended my gratitude to the many poets, artists and journalists who every September commemorated the Lares Rebellion and its rebels. I was particularly touched by the lyrical works of the late Juan Antonio Corretjer.

A generous grant from the Ford Foundation made it possible for me to support myself and to devote my time solely to the research of this topic for an entire year. Without this support my task would have undoubtedly been more difficult.

Among the individuals who helped me locate important documents was Hector Vazquez, then Director of the Puerto Rican Forum of New York City. He was kind enough to give me a xerox copy of an entire "pieza" of the Lares documents that had come into his possession many years earlier. His help is deeply appreciated.

I am also especially grateful to the many persons in the Puerto Rican archives who made my task easier by offering leads on documents that appeared outside the boxes I was reviewing. Among them, I would like to especially thank the archivists Eduardo Leon and Luis de la Rosa of the Archivo General de Puerto Rico. They, more than anyone, made my work a lot easier by taking the time to locate many unclassified papers that later proved enormously helpful to this work.

Among the many other persons I want to thank are Don Angel Vega, of the Archivo Municipal of Mayaguez, the staff of the Centro de Investigaciones Historicas at the University of Puerto Rico, at Rio Piedras, and the members of the archivo Historico Nacional and the Biblioteca Nacional of Spain in Madrid for their help in helping me to secure copies of documents related to the Grito de Lares and its rebels.

Outside of the academic world, I also incurred debts of gratitude with family and friends. My friends and colleagues Gloria Rodriguez and Israel Rivera went out of their way to make me feel at home by letting me share their apartment for several months while I carried out the research for the book. My sister Norma Jiménez took charge of my two young children for extended periods of time while I went back and forth between New Jersey and San Juan. How I could have done the research required for this book without her help is something I cannot imagine.

Finally, I would be remiss not to mention that without the encouragement and shared sacrifice of my husband Kal Wagenheim and our children David and Maria, the pursuit of my goals may have never materialized.

Olga Jiménez de Wagenheim
Maplewood, New Jersey
April 1993

Introduction

On 23 September 1868, between 600 and 1,000 men, the majority of them creoles from western Puerto Rico, rose in the town of Lares to demand independence from Spain. By midnight they had taken over the municipal seat of government, deposed the Spanish officials, and carried them off to jail along with the major Spanish merchants of the area. They declared Puerto Rico independent, installed a provisional government, abolished the *libreta* system, and offered freedom to any slave joining the rebel cause.

By the next afternoon, the rebels were routed by the militia of Pepino and pursued by the regular troops from Aguadilla and Arecibo. Having struck one week before the date agreed on, the rebels thought it would be best to wage a guerrilla war from the hills until other towns seconded their cry and their exiled leader Ramón E. Betances arrived with the ship, weapons, and recruits he had secured in Saint Thomas and Santo Domingo.

Neither plan materialized and with the ports closely watched by the Spanish soldiers the rebels found themselves trapped in hills that offered little cover. The untimely discovery of their plot had allowed the colonial authorities to put into operation a counterinsurgency plan that prevented the rebels from obtaining any outside support. Poorly armed and without aid or protection, the rebels were easily captured by the Spanish troops pursuing them.

Except for the 20 who managed to escape, the eight who died in action, and the seven who were summarily tried by the War Council, the majority of the insurgents were turned over to the civil courts. Four months later, the Spanish government, itself a product of a liberal takeover during the September 1868 revolution, freed all Puerto Rican prisoners by declaring a general amnesty. While no one was executed or kept in jail more than four months, 80 of the rebel prisoners died in jail from a yellow fever epidemic.

Yet, neither the short duration of the armed struggle nor the fact that the rebels failed to liberate the island has diminished the significance of the Grito de Lares. On the contrary, that historical event has grown in importance for an increasing number of Puerto Ricans since the 1930s. The founding leaders of the Nationalist Party declared the Grito de Lares a symbol of Puerto Rican identity and called upon the Puerto Ricans to pay tribute to the revolutionary patriots. Every year since the early 1930s thousands of islanders visit the town of Lares on 23 September to honor the Lares rebels.

In recent years, the Grito de Lares has also been recognized by government officials of various political views. For example, in 1969 Governor Luis A. Ferré, an advocate of statehood for Puerto Rico, declared 23 September a national holiday. Also, the Institute of Puerto Rican Culture, created by the government of the Commonwealth, declared Lares an historical site and placed a plaque in its plaza to commemorate the uprising.

Despite the present recognition of the importance of the Grito de Lares, there is only one book-length treatise devoted to it. This work was written four years after the uprising took place by José Pérez Moris, a loyalist Spaniard. His main purpose in recording the event was to discredit the revolutionaries and the Puerto Rican liberals who since the uprising had been petitioning Spain for reforms. The few other accounts of the Lares revolt that were written during the nineteenth century were the works of creole liberals who did their utmost to downplay its importance and scope before the Spanish officials. The fact that Puerto Rico remained a colony of Spain until 1898 may help to explain why pro-Lares literature did not appear until this century.

It was with the emergence of the Nationalist Party that a revisionist literature about the Grito de Lares was born. Essentially written by the political ideologues of the party and persons sympathetic to the liberation cause, the new literature identified Lares as the birthplace of Puerto Rican nationalism and the revolt as an example to be emulated. Caught between the devastating conditions of the economic depression of the 1930s and United States colonialism, the Nationalists sought to identify with the 1868 rebels.

In the following decades many articles and essays were written about the Lares revolt and the patriots who plotted it. Unfortunately, the majority of these writings are plagued by errors and generally lack the most basic documentation. Only a few of them were written by scholars. These, although generally documented, suffer from the tendency of viewing the Lares uprising as an extension of the biography of the revolutionary leaders who launched it. In particular, most of these works equate the revolt and its motives with the work of Ramón Emeterio Betances, the creole physician in exile who became the leader of the conspiracy. The motives and actions of the hundreds of creoles who went into the battlefield even though Betances could not join them were never discussed in any of these essays.

In the last eight years, the works of Ricardo Camuñas and Laird Bergad have followed a different path by studying the social and economic motives that produced the uprising. By focusing on the conditions of the society of Lares over a period of 20 years, the authors try to demonstrate that the revolt was local in scope and economically motivated. Bergad's work is a sophisticated socio-economic analysis of the Lares society that proves to be very valuable for understanding the local antagonisms that could have predisposed the creoles of that town to the revolutionary literature. Yet, by focusing strictly on the local conditions and the economic motives, Bergad has obscured the important role that was played by the revolutionary leaders in shaping the uprising. Thus his interpretation of the Lares revolt represents the other extreme of the purely political interpretation.

In this study we will attempt to close the gap between the material and the ideological interpretations by integrating them with several other factors that also contributed to shaping the forces that were unleashed in the uprising. It is our premise that the mere presence of either social antagonisms between the Spaniards and the creoles, or the appearance of political ideologues calling for revolution were not in themselves enough cause to lead the discontent into an armed confrontation. It should be remembered that Spain had a role to play in these matters and could have easily placated the creole dissidents by granting them the few reforms they requested in 1867. It should also be noted that between the urban revolutionary leaders and the hundreds of exploited creoles in the rural countryside there had to exist a connecting link that allowed them to work together toward a common goal.

Throughout this study I will try to answer the following questions: Why did the Lares uprising occur in 1868 and not decades earlier, when other Spanish American colonies went to war with Spain? What forces delayed the insurrectionary spirit in Puerto Rico? What were the specific as well as the general motives behind the Lares revolt? Who were the rebels who rose in Lares? Why did they fail to liberate the island? What impact did their actions have on the post insurrectionary relationships between the colony and the metropolis?

The research for this study was primarily done in the Archivo General de Puerto Rico (AGPR), the Archivo Municipal de Mayagüez (AMM), and the Centro de Investigaciones Históricas (CIH) of the University of Puerto Rico. Several documents were also obtained in microfilm from the Biblioteca Nacional de Cuba, and the Biblioteca and Archivo Histórico Nacional in Madrid. The bulk of the documentation for this work came from primary sources until now not used by other scholars. Months were spent reading through hundreds of testimonies given by the rebels when they were captured. Official correspondence between various judges, Audiencia, the office of the Governor and the military court were read and compared against other sources of information.

Among the municipal documents consulted the most useful were those of Lares, San Sebastián, and Camuy. The municipal documents of Mayagüez, although rich in content, are a nightmare to work with, for they were bound into book form without any classification whatsoever. Mayagüez also lacks the *Protocolos Notariales* (Notary Records) that were so helpful in the case of the other municipalities in tracing the social and economic standing of many of the rebels.

Several secondary sources were also used to establish the historical chronology up to the 1860s. The interpretation of well-known events such as the *Cédula de Gracias*, or the Reforms of Charles III are my contribution and not those of the authors, unless I specifically state otherwise. Of particular interest were the studies of several leading historians such as Salvador Brau, Lidio Cruz Monclova, Arturo Morales Carrión, Loida Figueroa, and Labor Gómez Acevedo. Of the specialized studies that proved invaluable were those of Fernando Picó, Francisco A. Scarano, Luis E. González Vales, Ricardo Camuñas, Laird Bergad, Estela Cifre de Loubriel, Astrid Iguina, among others. Relating to the Lares uprising, the best secondary source to date is still the 1872 work by José Pérez Moris.

This book is divided into five chapters and a conclusion. Chapter I describes the colonization up to the late eighteenth century and compares it with the same process in Spanish America. It analyzes the factors that delayed the insurrectionary stage in Puerto Rico and demonstrates that following the eruption of war in Spanish America, Spain accelerated its colonization of Puerto Rico via a series of reforms and imperial controls. By analyzing the colonial policies Spain adopted after the 1760s, the chapter explains the changes the society underwent and how the colony became increasingly more dependent on Spain.

Chapter II discusses the motives that led the rebels to declare war against Spain in 1868. It evaluates the rebel literature and extrapolates from it the many reasons the colony had to rebel against the metropolis. It also studies the social and economic standing of the rebel leaders and demonstrates that a great many of them were resentful of, as well as in debt to, the recently arrived immigrants, particularly the Spanish merchants.

Chapter III discusses the political conditions in the colony and contrasts them with the aspirations of the creoles and the ever present promises by Spain. It describes the unfulfilled promises of 1867 and the exile of the liberal intellectuals as the catalytic agents that led to the decision among some of them that Puerto Rico would be better off without Spain. It traces also the steps taken by the revolutionary movement and the counterinsurgency plan developed by the government.

Chapter IV explains how the conspiracy was betrayed and revises the explanation offered by José Pérez Moris. It states the reasons and preparations that led to the change of date of the attack. It describes, in detail, the attack on Lares and corrects a number of errors of the more traditional literature. It analyzes the actions of the provisional rebel government and demonstrates that its program was inadequate to attract support from several sectors of the creole society.

Chapter V focuses on the capture and legal proceedings of the rebels, the struggles over the prisoners between the civil and military courts, the testimonies given by the insurgents, and the outcomes of the sentences. It discusses the treatment of the prisoners by the civil and military authorities and explains why Spain, through its representative in Puerto Rico, decided to end the proceedings with a generous amnesty for all.

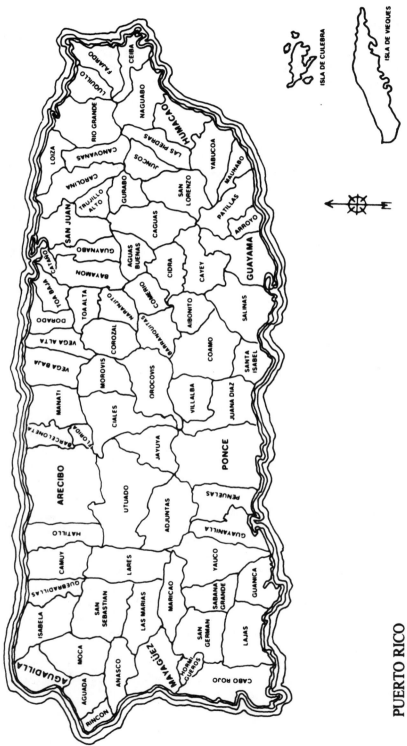

PUERTO RICO

Courtesy of Puerto Rico's Government Development Bank

I
The "New" Colonization:
A Profile of Puerto Rico

The Napoleonic invasion of Spain in 1808 did not result in a cry for independence in Puerto Rico as it did in the majority of the Spanish American colonies. Puerto Rico, like Cuba, remained under Spanish colonial rule until the end of the nineteenth century, despite its attempt to liberate itself in 1868. Ironically, for Puerto Rico, the Napoleonic invasion of Spain resulted in a "new" colonization and greater royal controls.

To understand why the island remained a colony, after Spanish America won its independence, and why it did not challenge Spanish sovereignty until 1868, it is necessary to review the history of the "old" colony as well as the changes that were introduced by the "new" colonial policy adopted by Spain.

The "Old" Colony

Both Puerto Rico and Spanish America were colonized by Spain during the sixteenth century, but as colonies they were not equally developed nor used for the same purposes. Puerto Rico, unlike Spanish South America, was primarily used as a military outpost until the end of the eighteenth century. Lacking the mineral wealth and large indigenous population of Mexico or Peru, Puerto Rico became valuable to Spain for its strategic position in the West Indies. The island's size and location made it possible for Spain to fortify it and use it to patrol the Caribbean and to protect its colonies to the South. In all other sectors, Puerto Rico remained essentially neglected by the royal government until the late eighteenth century.

England's occupation of Havana in 1763, the loss of needed trade revenues to contraband, and the Bourbons' desire to regain the old glory of Spain led to a reorganization of the Spanish empire in the 1760s. The new royal policy implanted by Charles III sought to regain control of the colonies by strengthening their colonial ties and heightening their dependency on Spain. That imperial policy was gradually extended to Puerto Rico as well.

In 1765, a royal agent, Marshal Alejandro O'Reilly, was sent to Puerto Rico by Charles III to report on the island's conditions and to recommend measures for its future development.

1

O'Reilly's study[1] reported that the island had only 44,883 persons, of which 5,037 were slaves. These lived scattered throughout the island, far from the seat of government and church. The settlers also preferred to live far away from one another in the rural countryside. As he put it:

> In the towns, the capital included, there are few permanent inhabitants besides the curate; the others are always in the country, except Sundays and feast days, when those living near a church come to hear mass.

He was appalled by the general ignorance of the settlers. The social customs and the conditions in which they lived were summarized by O'Reilly:

> To form an idea of how these natives live, it is enough to say that there are only two schools on the island; that outside of the capital and San Germán few know how to read; that they count time by changes in the government, hurricanes, (and) visits from bishops. . . . The principal ones among them, including those of the capital, when in the country, go barefooted and barelegged . . .

The island's economy was basically undeveloped, depending on subsistence farming and illegal trade with the United States and the European colonies in the Caribbean. The neglect of the island's potential for commercial agriculture and the entrenched illicit trade failed to create in Puerto Rico the wealthy class of creole landowners found in other Spanish colonies. Nor were there the great haciendas and colonial mansions found in Mexico or Perú at the end of the eighteenth century. In describing the homes of the Puerto Rican settlers, O'Reilly said:

> They occupy houses that look like hen coops, consisting of a couple of rooms, most of them without windows or doors and therefore open day and night. Their furniture is so scant that they can move in an instant . . .

He summarized the state of the economy when he said:

> There are no markets, no internal trade, and not one-twentieth of the land distributed has been cleared for cultivation.

To make the colony a valuable possession to the Crown, O'Reilly concluded that the practice of granting land to the poor was not the solution, as that only encouraged their dispersion and increased their rusticity. Instead, he recommended that all the uncultivated land be returned to the Crown, so that such land could be distributed to farmers willing to plant it. He suggested that a tax be levied on those farms given in ownership to encourage landowners to plant their land. He reasoned that the revenues from the land tax could be used to help defray the cost of the military forces and to pay for repairs needed by the fortifications.[2]

O'Reilly appeared optimistic about the future of the colony provided its agriculture was commercially developed and its administration were revamped and brought under closer imperial scrutiny. To achieve these ends, the island had to increase its population, reorganize its defense system, and obtain a more flexible trade policy from Spain. The colony needed urgent economic reforms that would allow it to acquire revenues to support itself.

Beginning in the mid-1760s Puerto Rico was earmarked for some of the Bourbon reforms. Gradually, the royal government extended a number of social and economic measures to stimulate productivity and curb contraband trade. Immigration rules were relaxed and incentives were provided to attract new settlers. Prospective immigrants from Catholic nations in Europe and the Caribbean were encouraged to settle in Puerto Rico during the rest of the eighteenth century. A few trade concessions wrested from Spain during this period lured some French planters from war-torn Saint Domingue to grow sugar and coffee in Puerto Rico. The temporary trade measures helped the settlers to secure slaves and work tools needed to boost agricultural production.[3]

Thus, compared to Spanish America, Puerto Rico at the end of the eighteenth century was just beginning its colonization. In 1797 the population of the colony was approximately 158,000 persons. Its agriculture awaited better incentives. The annual revenues collected, a mere 60,000 pesos, were not enough to cover the costs of the colonial administration.[4]

Consequently, in Puerto Rico, the Bourbon reforms did not produce the antagonistic clashes that in Spanish America prepared the road for the wars of independence. The island simply had not attained the level of social and economic development John Lynch found in Mexico and Spanish South America.[5] Nor did Puerto Rico have a wealthy class of creoles used to sharing power with the colonial administration. Hence, it was not in a position to challenge the metropolis at the beginning of the nineteenth century as the other colonies did. In Puerto Rico, contrary to what happened in Spanish South America, the new imperial policy began by Spain in the 1760s merely set the stage for what we have called the "new" colonization of Puerto Rico. It is this reconquest of the island in the eighteenth century and the following colonization that delayed the insurrectionary spirit in Puerto Rico until the mid-nineteenth century.

The "New" Colony

Following Napoleon's occupation of Spain, a ruling junta representing the Spanish government in Cadiz and granted Puerto Rico the right to hold its first colonial elections, to choose a delegate who could represent the island in Spain. The person elected, Ramón Power y Giralt, worked hard during the years 1810 to 1812 to convince the ruling Junta in Cadiz to extend to Puerto Rico some of the liberal reforms they were considering for Spain.[6]

Upon Power's recommendations, the Cortes appointed the island's first intendant, Alejandro Ramírez, in 1812. The new intendant was to administer the island's financial and economic affairs, which until then had been under the jurisdiction of the captain-general.[7] The economy was in crisis. The removal of the *situado* (a royal subsidy sent from the Mexican Treasury) and the devalued paper money, printed by the governor to cover expenses, unleashed a severe inflation and devaluation of the paper currency. Ramírez' first task was complex; he had to withdraw the paper money from circulation, balance the colonial budget, and secure the funds to support the administration.

Between 1813 and 1816, Ramírez implanted a number of measures that ended the economic crisis and set the structure for its development. Gradually, he removed the paper money from circulation and increased the use of the metallic currency from South America. He founded a state lottery, reformed the tax system, and encouraged agricultural production.

Commercial agriculture was protected and encouraged through a series of incentives. Export duties were reduced while some imports, farm tools, machinery, and slaves, were brought in duty free during some years.

During Ramírez' intendancy, the journal *El Diario Económico* began publication and the *Sociedad Económica de Amigos del País* was founded. Both organs helped to disseminate the latest scientific information on agriculture and industry among the colonists of Puerto Rico throughout the better part of the nineteenth century.[8]

The liberal reforms implemented by Intendant Ramirez helped to create in Puerto Rico the economic infrastructure that would permit colonial development. With the restoration of Ferdinand VII to the Spanish throne, the island was extended other reforms, known collectively as the *Real Cédula de Gracias* (1815-1836). For twenty years the reforms granted by that royal decree provided many incentives to old and new settlers to transform the rural economy from one of subsistence farming into one of commercial crops for export.[9]

At a time when South America was fighting Spain for its independence, the Crown found it desirable to shower Puerto Rico with favors. Coming so soon after the Ramírez' reforms, those of the Cédula de Gracias gave the economy the push that would launch it into a period of economic prosperity.

Although the prosperity was short-lived, the reforms set a precedent in the colonists' view, namely that for the colony to prosper it must remain tied to Spain. The evident results of the reforms also raised expectations among the creoles which no colonial policy could fulfill.

Yet, the purposes of the 1815 reforms were no different from those of the old Bourbon reforms: to increase the value of the colony and to preserve it under Spanish control. To insure these, generous conditions were provided for loyal exiles from war-torn Spanish America to relocate to Puerto Rico. Their presence, in time, would serve a double purpose: it would help increase the island's population and help to neutralize any liberal political sentiments the creoles may have entertained.

The practice of granting sporadic economic concessions and silencing the pro-independence sentiments in Puerto Rico became particularly entrenched after the 1820s. Following the loss of Spanish America and the death of Ferdinand VII in the 1830s, Puerto Rico was once again relegated to a plain colonial status. Gone were the concessions and reforms the island had come to depend on. Without these special protective measures, the colonial economy stagnated around the 1850s. By then, however, the colony was highly militarized and under the firm grip of a conservative captain-general. Colonial trade was in Spanish hands and the administration of the colony was reserved for a growing Spanish bureaucracy. It was against these conditions that hundreds of creoles revolted in Lares in September 1868. For what John Lynch said of Spanish America following the reforms of the 1760s came to pass in Puerto Rico nearly a century later.

> (Spain's) reformism whetted appetites which it could not satisfy, while (its) imperialism mounted a direct attack on local interests and disturbed the delicate balance of power within the colony.[10]

To understand how the new colonial policy unleashed the forces that would result in an armed confrontation with Spain, we will review the general conditions of the colony between 1815 and 1868. The specific motives that drove hundreds of creoles to revolt in Lares are addressed in another chapter.

The Economy

The reforms extended by the Cédula de Gracias helped to liberalize the trade between Puerto Rico and Spain.[11] For fifteen years the island could engage in *comercio libre* (free trade) with Spain, provided the goods were transported in Spanish ships. The island could also trade with the remaining Spanish colonies in the New World, at a reduced tax rate of 2 percent.

The colony was also authorized to trade with foreign nations, friendly to Spain, for a period of fifteen years, at a low rate of 6 percent. Goods from foreign nations, however, were to be imported when they could not be secured in Spain. To avoid competition for local export products, sugar, molasses, rum, and tobacco were protected by the Crown.

Developed as an agrarian economy, the colony was dependent on manufactured goods from outside sources. These could be imported from foreign
nations so long as they paid a 15 percent tax. Farm equipment and industrial
machinery were the exception, and paid between 2 and 3 percent import
tax. The lowest rate was reserved for goods carried in Spanish bottoms.

Trade with the nearby Caribbean nations, while generally discouraged,
was authorized during cases of emergency. For example, after the 1817
Anglo-Spanish treaty that promised to end the slave trade, the colonists of
Puerto Rico purchased many of the slaves they needed in the Caribbean
nations. Trade with the Caribbean islands was subject to a variable tax rate,
which ranged from 3 to 5 percent on imports and 5 percent on colonial
exports. The low 3 percent tax was applied to the slaves imported.

The liberalization of the trade led to an increase in the volume of trade
between the island and other nations, including Spain. Between 1816 and
1834 the value of the trade carried out in the colony increased from 1,082,299
to 7,892,166 pesos. By 1844 that sum had risen to 11,462,054 pesos.[12]
Yet, the increase in traffic did not benefit the creoles as much as it did the
Spanish merchants. The reciprocal trade agreements made possible by
comercio libre allowed the Spanish merchants to introduce into Puerto Rico
a lot more goods, namely manufactured and processed expensive goods,
than the island could export to Spain.

For example, by 1844 the colony was already experiencing a balance of
trade deficit. That year it imported over one million pesos more than it
received for its exports. By 1864 the negative trade differential for the island
had grown to over six million pesos. Similarly, the trade statistics of the
colony between 1862 and 1872 reveal that the island was spending twice as
much for its imports as it was receiving for its exports. More than 40 percent
of the sum spent on imports went to pay for agrarian products that a few
years before had been produced in Puerto Rico.[13]

The combined effects of a colonial policy that reserved the best lands for
commercial agriculture, and a fast growing population left the colony little
choice but to continue to import the needed staples. Of the 68,000 *cuerdas*
(1 cuerda = 0.9412 acre) placed under cultivation between 1830 and 1862
84 percent were devoted to commercial crops for export and 14 percent were
planted in food crops.[14]

Foods such as rice, flour, lard, and dried codfish had been traditionally
imported from Spain's competitors at considerable savings during the years
of contraband trade. With the legalization of the trade the Spanish market was protected, but shipping costs increased and the price of food-
stuffs rose beyond the reach of the laboring classes.[15] In Lares in 1866
codfish sold for 8 *centavos* a pound and lard for 24 centavos while the
wage paid to a *jornalero* for a day's work ranged from 2 to 4 *reales*, or 10
to 20 centavos.[16]

Despite the long-range problems of dependency and deficit in the balance of trade produced by comercio libre, the creoles continued to ask for it during the rest of the nineteenth century. For the creole planters, in particular, the liberalized trade of the Cédula de Gracias granted a needed incentive, as they were generally hardpressed to compete with other planters for the foreign markets. Devoid of credit institutions, short of cash and labor, and without much possibility of obtaining modern machinery, they were grateful to Spain for any concessions.

Yet while Spain was not eager to reduce the colonial dependency, it was not always able to grant trade reforms nor to help its economy by purchasing its products. Of the total value of Puerto Rico's exports in 1866, Spain purchased about 828,932 *escudos* (about 500,000 pesos) worth of goods, compared to more than 8 million escudos purchased by the United States, England and foreign nations in the Caribbean (see Table I).

In general, the liberalization of the trade was sporadic and only partially helpful. It made possible the curtailment of illegal trade and the collection of customs revenues needed by the local treasury. But, as the new revenues increased, so did the colonial bureaucracy. Thus, new funds which should have been used to provide services, to build public works and roads were generally spent on salaries for Spanish officials. Yet, for the peninsulares, as merchants, shippers, and money-lenders, the liberal trade concessions served to penetrate the colonial market, which by the 1850s had taken them into the interior of Puerto Rico. There, they would struggle with the creoles

TABLE I

Partial value of Puerto Rico's external trade, in escudos, and its most important trade partners, 1866*

	Imports	Exports
Spain	4,847,019	828,932
United States	3,714,315	5,957,690
Non-Hispanic Caribbean	3,246,795	749,421
England	2,510,858	1,570,812
Sub-Total	14,317,087	9,106,855

Source: United States, Consular Despatches, Alexander Jourdan to William H. Seward, Enclosure with Despatch No. 104.

*The Total trade value that year was 28,279,141 escudos, of which 17,256,961 escudos were spent on imports and 11,022,180 were received for the Island's exports.

and recently arrived immigrants mainly from South America and Corsica for the few administrative jobs, the incipient commercial avenues, and the much coveted land.

More than trade, the provisions of the Cédula de Gracias sought to promote agriculture. While the emphasis was placed on commercial crops, the decree also envisioned the emergence of a class of small farmers. To that end, free land gifts and tax exemptions were given to prospective immigrants willing to settle in Puerto Rico and devote themselves to agriculture. For example, any white immigrant farmer who met these qualifications and accepted the Spanish King and Catholic faith could obtain about six acres of land for each family member and half that amount for each slave he brought into the country. Mulattoes and free blacks with the same qualifications were given one half the land granted to whites. White settlers were also exempted from several taxes, including the *alcábala* (sales tax) and the tithe, for fifteen years. Mulattoes and free blacks were basically extended the same privileges, but only for five years.[17]

With these and other incentives, land cultivation in Puerto Rico gradually increased, from 120,721 cuerdas in 1830 to 189,000 in 1862.[18] Most of the land placed under cultivation was devoted to the growing of the major crops coffee and sugar. Virgin soil, greater use of fertilizers, and the combined labor force of slaves and laborers helped to increase production and to bring more acres under cultivation. Sugar, the most important export crop until the 1870s, increased production from 18 million pounds in 1828 to 100 million pounds in 1849. A less dramatic increase was registered during the decade of 1850, as production figures oscillated between 112 million and 116 million pounds between 1850 and 1860.[19]

High demand, good prices, and easier access to the United States market, while the Cédula de Gracias was in effect, led many farmers to turn to the cultivation of sugar cane. Between 1828 and 1862 the land devoted to sugar increased threefold, expanding from 14,803 cuerdas to 55,941 cuerdas.[20]

By the middle of the century, however, the sugar industry was already experiencing a number of problems, which 30 years later would force it to lose its primary role in the colonial economy. A chronic shortage of cash, limited credit facilities, decreasing fertility of the soil, a sudden decline in sugar prices and demand, and the termination of the slave trade by Spain in 1845 made it difficult for most sugar growers to survive. As Francisco A. Scarano has so ably demonstrated, in Ponce only the large sugar hacendados, who were generally recently arrived immigrants, were able to withstand the tough times, often at the expense of the creole growers.[21]

While coffee had not been singled out for protection by the provisions of the Cédula de Gracias, it managed to attain a secondary position in the export economy of the island during the first six decades of the nineteenth century. By the last quarter of the century, it had surpassed the sugar industry in the export value it produced for Puerto Rico.[22] Much of the success of this industry had to do with the growing demand for the bean in Europe, the steady purchases by Spain and Cuba, and the settling of the island's interior, where the soil was ideal for coffee cultivation. The arrival of the Spanish merchants in the interior after 1848 was also very important to the industry, as they provided credit to the planters and improved the marketing of the coffee crops.

Introduced initially in the 1750s, coffee cultivation spread relatively fast during the eighteenth century, becoming an item of contraband by 1765. By 1783, the island exported over one million pounds of coffee to Europe.[23]

During the first half of the nineteenth century coffee grew less dramatically than sugar, as it was a product of the hinterlands which were just being populated. By 1828, coffee production in Puerto Rico had reached 11 million pounds. This figure, however, was surpassed only four times in the following 12 years. During the decade of 1850 the coffee industry produced between 9 and 13 million pounds a year.[24] But, by 1863, when the sugar industry began to stagnate, coffee production began a slow, steady climb, becoming by the 1890s the best value producing export crop.

The land devoted to coffee production also increased during these years, expanding from 17,247 cuerdas in 1830 to 33,965 cuerdas in 1862. By 1896 the land used by the coffee growers had increased to 122,000 cuerdas, or 105,000 more than in 1830. By contrast, the land devoted to sugar cultivation had increased by only 47,000 cuerdas between 1830 and 1896.[25]

Increasing prices and a growing demand for the island's coffee led to a period of prosperity for the interior of Puerto Rico. Yet such prosperity did not benefit all those involved in coffee production. As the cases of Lares and Utuado demonstrate, the expansion of the coffee industry often led to the impoverishment of the small and medium-sized farmers, many of whom lost their plots due to debts.[26] Short of cash, the small *hacendados* were unable to expand production without contracting large debts with the Spanish merchants of their municipalities. These, in due time, foreclosed on them and took over their properties.

For the landless workers, the expansion of the coffee industry generally meant a restriction of their freedom, as they were prohibited from squatting on public or private land and forced to work for the hacendados. By virtue of the labor regulations imposed after 1848, the free laboring classes were coerced to work for the hacendados or face punishment. As the best lands of the interior were monopolized by the coffee planters, less cuerdas were were used for foodcrops and the diet of the workers worsened.[27] The concentration of the land by the coffee planters also pushed up the price of the cuerda out of reach of most laborers. For example, the average price of a cuerda in Lares between 1835 and 1840 was 4.9 pesos. The same cuerda cost about 7.3 pesos between 1841 and 1850 and 37.64 pesos in 1868.[28] Thus any hopes the laborer may have had of buying land were quickly frustrated by the skyrocketing prices. Landless, without skills, and without any education, they were condemned to a life of work that did not even pay enough to cover their basic needs.

The economic reforms extended by Spain in the nineteenth century did not encourage colonial self-sufficiency. Manufacturing was generally discouraged by the imposition of high import duties on raw materials and machinery for that purpose.

Industry was primarily limited to sugar cane and its derivatives, such as molasses, sugar and rum. The development of other industries was prevented by means of legislation and high taxes favorable to Spain. A chronic shortage of metallic currency and the lack of banking and credit institutions compounded the problem. Thus, the colony after 50 years of Spanish efforts had few shops and factories and depended on the overseas trade for its manufactured and processed goods.

By the 1860s the Puerto Rican economy had gradually changed from subsistence farming toward commercial agriculture. But, as commercial farming grew, the island came to experience other problems which could not be easily resolved. For example, the small farmers became indebted, the landless workers were pauperized, and the island became more dependent than ever on the overseas trade. As the colony consumed more than it exported, its economy was increasingly decapitalized. Of the 28,000,000 escudos produced by the island's trade in 1866 over 17,000,000 were spent by the colony to pay for its imports.

In 1867, the economic problems were further complicated by a hurricane in October and earth tremors from November until January. While we do not have figures for the damages they caused, letters from Lares and Mayagüez make it evident that the economy that year suffered a setback. The syndic of Mayagüez, Manuel María Mangual, reported to the Governor of Puerto Rico that due to the hurricane the crops that year would not be enough to even satisfy the cash loans the farmers had contracted with the merchants to operate their farms.[29] Referring to the sugar hacendados' plight, he said:

Las haciendas de caña, de la producción la más valiosa y una de las que más contribuye al sostenimiento de las necesidades en general, y ya en esperas de romper molienda, alcanzarán tan sólo a indemnizar las pérdidas (sufridas).

Many of the poor persons of Mayagüez, he said, were left homeless and destitute:

(El) huracán que el 29 de Octubre nos ha visitado. . . . ha arrazado los campos, ha producido corrientes extraordinarias, (en las que) muchas víctimas han encontrado su sepelio. . . . El viento ha destruido infinitos cacerías dejando a la inclemencia a miles de infelices. . . .

After detailing the state of the Mayagüez economy and the woes of the local planters, Sr. Mangual requested from the Governor a two year tax exmption for the municipality.

From Lares, Mariana Bracetti also wrote to the Governor, on a personal matter.[30] She reported the destruction caused by the hurricanes on her farm and explained the difficulties this brought to her household, as her husband was a sick man and her only son was crippled. Without the food crops, and with the meager income she made from sewing, there would not be enough to support her large family. Given these circumstances, she hoped that his excellency would let her keep her slave, Marcos, whom she hired out to a bakery in Añasco.

Whether the Governor helped Mariana is hard to say, but he definitely did not agree to the request of Sr. Mangual. On the contrary, Mayagüez was admonished for trying to get away with not meeting its responsibilities to the royal treasury. Since the colonial coffers were bare, Mayagüez was asked to pay in advance one fourth of the taxes due in July 1868.

In short, by 1867 the economy of Puerto Rico was in crisis and the colonial officials were in no position to help. Spain was unable or unwilling to extend more concessions and many creoles were discontented. While economic troubles in themselves were not enough for the rebels of Lares to take up arms against Spain, they certainly contributed to their decision when they realized that Spain would not help.

The Administration

Relations between Puerto Rico and Spain changed relatively little during the greater part of the nineteenth century, as the island was kept as a colony, subjected to the government of the metropolis. There were exceptions, however, and during the first two constitutional governments in Spain (1812-14, 1820-23) the island was granted political concessions and administrative changes that led to increased expectations among the creoles.

Following the adoption of the 1812 Constitution, the ruling junta of Cadiz changed the status of Puerto Rico from one of colony to one of province. As a result of the new status, all the free inhabitants of the island were permitted limited representation in the Spanish cortes and some participation in the affairs of the colony. The question of representation became a problem for the metropolis which did not want to extend the same privileges and rights to the various groups in the colony that it was extending to the citizens in Spain.[31] Thus, it revised the laws and bypassed the thorny issue of proportional representation by differentiating between Spaniards and citizens. Spaniards were all free persons born in Spain or its colonies, but citizens were only those Spaniards who could trace both their parents' ancestry, to Spain. Only the citizens thus classified were entitled to the rights and privileges enjoyed by Spaniards in Spain. For example, they could take part in local elections, when they were called, be elected to public offices, be represented, and represent the island before the Spanish officials in Spain.

Other concessions granted during these liberal years included a partial decentralization of the colonial administration. At the executive level, the first office of intendant was created in 1812 to separate the fiscal obligations from the office of the captain-general. Similarly, in 1822, the civil and military powers were separated by the creation of a new post for a civil governor. During both constitutional periods, the executive power was further trimmed by the establishment of a nine member provincial council (Diputación Provincial) which was to share the job of administering the island with the governor.[32]

The political climate improved and the civil rights of the citizens were respected. Freedom of the press, speech, and assembly led to open discussions about the island's problems and to increasing petitions to the Spanish government. Jobs in the colonial administration became a possibility for the creoles for the first time since the island became a colony. Representation in the Cortes was expected to lead to greater decentralization of the government and possibly to political autonomy. At least that is what is reflected by the petitions made by the delegates from Puerto Rico during the 1820s and 1830s.

Their hopes, however, were soon shattered, for Spain cancelled all the reforms when it came under Ferdinand's absolute rule once again. Beginning in 1822, the King, engaged in war against Spanish America, subjected Puerto Rico again to military rule. He appointed governors who were primarily military generals and endowed them with unlimited powers to arrest, jail, or exile anyone suspected of harboring separatist thoughts. Although technically these governors obeyed royal orders, they generally ruled by decrees.

The first to hold such a post, after the political concessions ended, was Don Miguel de la Torre, a military general who had been defeated by Simón Bolivar's forces in Venezuela. De la Torre's administration paved the way for other more despotic governors that were to follow. He began a discrediting campaign against democracy, revolutionary principles, and rebel Spanish America. He tried to persuade the islanders that rape, hunger, terror, and anarchy would befall the colony if it tried to cut its ties with Spain. To boost his arguments, he strengthened the island's defense system and developed a spy network. To keep abreast of problems and developments in the island, he revived the *visitas*, or inspection tours. Permanent municipal boards, or *juntas de visitas*, were also established during his administration. Their function was to report to him any unusual developments in the island's towns. They also served as host groups anytime the governor or other officials went to tour the municipalities.[33]

Despite his surveillance, de la Torre was more careful than other governors not to antagonize the creoles unnecessarily. He appealed to the leading class because he encouraged development, ordered the construction of several public works, and aided the planter class by increasing the slave population.[34] De la Torre, however, had the advantage of ruling during years of growth and economic prosperity which were ushered in by the concessions of the Cédula de Gracias. As the economic reforms disappeared and the island came to experience harder times, the authorities resorted to harsher methods to keep the leading classes under control.

Between 1837 and 1868, political conditions in the colony became particularly oppressive. Deprived of representation, the creoles had little chance of participating in the affairs of the colony. Civil government became more centralized in a few Spanish hands, as the governor and his appointed officials controlled nearly everything. At the municipal level, the power of the *ayunta-mientos* (town councils) was severely limited by the fact that the mayor and the *teniente a guerra* (a delegate of the governor) were appointed by the governor as his representatives. Their function was to oversee the actions of the town councils. The teniente a guerra, in particular, as a representative of the governor, was empowered to head all ayuntamiento meetings. His recommendations were to be accepted at all times. The governor, however, reserved the right to veto any project the ayuntamiento proposed. All municipal decisions had to be approved by the governor as well.[35]

At all levels the society was subjected to many restrictions and widespread censorship. By the mid-1860s the inhabitants of the colony were forbidden to hold meetings, dances, and social gatherings unless these had been approved by the government. Anyone who dared to challenge the system was arrested, fined, and perhaps even jailed. No one could move about after curfew (generally set at 9 p.m.), change residence, read prohibited books, or publish anything the government considered offensive. For every one of these written permission had to be secured.[36]

Such surveillance and paperwork required added personnel. Thus, the civil bureaucracy and the military forces were greatly expanded after the 1830s. Following the loss of the Spanish American colonies the island was used to house hundreds of jobless Spanish officials fleeing from Spanish America. Cuba and Puerto Rico were expected to employ them until they could retire to Spain.

In the late 1840s a new wave of Spanish immigrants also came to Puerto Rico in search of economic opportunities. These, by virtue of their citizenship, were given priority over the creoles in the colonial administration. In Lares, for example, by the late 1840s recently arrived Spaniards were holding municipal posts previously held by creoles. The benefits accrued by these posts, such as the right to distribute municipal land, sell licenses, and distribute the taxes were lost to the creoles. Some Spaniards, with access to credit sources and the larger commercial houses, became merchants in their own right and thus deprived the creoles of another source of economic revenues.[37]

With war raging in Spanish America, the militarization of Puerto Rico regained momentum. The island's strategic importance was emphasized. The armed troops were increased and the militia was reorganized. After 1817, an old law was revived and it became obligatory for every male 16 years old and over to register for militia service. The island was divided into four military districts, or *comandancias*, from which troops could be dispatched to insurgent Spanish America.[38]

Increasing the military troops served a double purpose: it would facilitate the movement of the armed forces destined for Spanish America and would help deter any separatist movement that may be growing in Puerto Rico. Fear of invasion by Simón Bolivar's forces kept the authorities on the alert for many years. Later, the expansion of the military was justified by the unrest in the Caribbean and the many slave conspiracies uncovered in Puerto Rico. The restoration war in Santo Domingo (1861-64) and the abolitionist ferment generated in Puerto Rico by the emancipation of the slaves in the Caribbean and the United States also contributed to the government's rationale for adding five militia units in the 1860s.

The military expansion put a strain on the colonial budget and at times the soldier's salaries could not be paid. When this happened the governor became more fearful of the soldiers than of the creoles. By 1865, nearly 43 percent of the island's budget was spent on the military. The portion of the budget allocated to this group had increased from 100,000 pesos in 1815 to over 1.5 million pesos in 1865.[39]

Growing expenses at home were not the only burden the creoles had to contend with during the greater part of the century. Spain's continuous wars also became a drain on the island's meager resources, as the Crown demanded contributions for its war efforts. In 1821, for example, the island was required to donate 12,000 pesos to tend to the needs of hundreds of exiles from Venezuela who arrived in San Juan.[40] The forced contributions continued to increase with every war Spain fought abroad. By the 1860s Puerto Rico contributed in a five year period close to one million pesos for the Spanish wars in Morocco and in Santo Domingo. The contribution to the war in Santo Domingo included men and medical supplies as well as cash.[41]

The wars, however, were not the only reason for Spain to demand contributions. As Spain became more heavily indebted to foreign lenders, it expected its colonies to share the burden. Thus, in October 1865, Spain announced to Cuba and Puerto Rico that beginning in January 1866 they would be responsible for paying the interest on Spain's public debt.[42]

The practice of forced loans and "voluntary" contributions was also becoming entrenched on the island during the 1860s, as the governors could not generate enough revenues to cover the colonial expenses. For example, between August 1864 and January 1865 the colonial coffers were so bare that the governor forced the municipal councils to lend him their savings. The amounts borrowed ranged from 12,000 to 50,000 pesos a month. By July 1865 he had outstanding obligations which required a loan from the ayuntamiento of San Juan. The sum of 103,000 pesos which the ayuntamiento had been saving to construct an aqueduct for the city was taken by the governor to pay the soldiers and cover general expenses.[43]

Similar loans were exacted by the military officers of the districts from the rural towns of the island. According to one angry citizen from Arecibo, Colonel Manuel de Iturriaga had borrowed and squandered the money the ayuntamiento had been saving to put gas lights in the city.[44]

Besides these contributions and loans, the islanders had to pay an increasing number of taxes. These generally included the *subsidio* (income tax), *culto y clero* (church tax), the stamp tax, the consumption tax, and the *primicias*, or taxes levied for special projects. There were state taxes, municipal taxes, and church taxes. The municipal taxes were assigned in accordance with the needs of the town in any given year. The state taxes levied on the municipalities varied according to their production and importance.[45] Both the state and the municipal government called for "voluntary" contributions for the upkeep of the roads and the construction of public works. The proprietors, generally, fulfilled this obligation by sending hired jornaleros in their place. The jornaleros met their obligation by providing personal service. In 1865, the contributions for these works by the proprietors amounted to 600,000 pesos and those of the jornaleros to another 300,000 pesos.[46]

In short, the political and administrative reforms granted during these constitutional periods were revoked as soon as Spain returned to monarchical absolute rule. But in exposing the colony to better times the reforms helped to feed illusions among the creoles that Spain was unable to satisfy. When the rights and privileges were withdrawn the creoles petitioned the Crown, but when it failed to respond in a positive manner, some of them began to conspire against Spain. For example, in 1838 a number of creoles collaborated with a sector of the military troops of San Juan in a conspiracy to revolt, just after the island was denied representation in the Spanish Cortes that had been reopened by a new constitutional regime.[47] Similarly, the Lares uprising of 1868 came after the island was subjected to more unfulfilled promises by another liberal regime in Spain.

The Population and the Society

In forty-five years, the population of Puerto Rico more than doubled, from 220,892 in 1815 to 583,508 in 1860.[48] Natural reproduction, immigration, and importation of several thousand slaves contributed to the population expansion. From 1815 to 1834, the population of the colony increased by nearly 38 percent, or 137,944 persons. Of those, Colonel Flinter reported that nearly 10,000 were immigrants, 7,000 of them Spaniards from Venezuela and Santo Domingo and the others were naturalized foreigners from various nations.[49]

From 1834 to 1869 the colonial population grew by over 40 percent, from 358,836 to 600,233 persons (see Table II). Of the 1869 population, 96 percent were born in Puerto Rico, over 2 percent were born in Spain, and the rest were born in foreign nations. Five thousand of those foreign-born were slaves brought over from Africa.

TABLE II
Population increases, by race, Puerto Rico, 1834-1869

	1834	1846	1869
Total Population	358,836	443,139	600,233
White Population			
Total	188,869	216,083	323,454
Increases	—	27,216	107,371
Free Colored Population			
Total	126,399	175,791	237,710
Increases	—	49,392	61,919
Slave Population			
Total	41,818	51,265	39,069
Increases	—	9,447	−12,196

Sources: The figures for 1834 and 1846 appear in Carroll, *Report*, p. 200. Those for 1869 were taken from José Pérez Moris, *Historia de la Insurrección de Lares*, p. 242.

According to the racial breakdown given by the censuses of 1834, 1846, and 1869, the free colored population grew almost twice as fast as the white population between 1834 and 1846, but experienced a relative decline in growth between 1846 and 1869. During the first period, the free colored group increased by 49,392 individuals, while the white group increased by only 27,216 persons (see Table II). The slave population during this same period grew by 9,447 individuals, but during the second period suffered a loss of 12,196 persons. In the second period, the free colored group grew by 61,919 persons while the white population increased by 107,371 persons.

Why the black population lost its lead over the white population after the 1840s was probably due as much to restrictive colonial measures as to accidental factors. Although many creoles and colonial administrators tried to attract white settlers when they could, the fact was that until the late 1840s conditions beyond their control forced them to accept free colored persons from the Caribbean. Limited resources with which to purchase slaves, increasing restrictions on the slave trade, and the growing need for workers in the sugar industry pushed the colonial government to open the doors to free black workers from the nearby Caribbean islands. Prospective free black farmers were also lured by the land grants offered by the Cédula de Gracias.

By the late 1840s, however, conditions in Puerto Rico had changed, making the island less attractive to free blacks, laborers in particular. The economic crisis of the sugar industry beginning in 1848 and the strict labor regulations that followed in 1849 kept many of the prospective migrant workers away. The abolition of the slave trade and the lack of incentives to free persons of color to obtain land reduced their numbers as well. Poverty, malnutrition and periodic epidemics contributed to the reduction of the black population during some years.[50]

The fact that blacks were still numerous was used by the conservative Spaniards to plant fear in the society. For example, in 1872, the editor of the *Boletín Mercantil* warned the creoles that if the Spanish government was forced out of Puerto Rico, the island would immediately lose about 100,000 white persons and the blacks would be in majority. They would then take over the government. If they could not take over peacefully, they would resort to racial war, as in Haiti, or would intimidate those in government, as was the case in the southern United States.[51] The warning was directed at the Puerto Rican separatists, who in 1868 had attracted hundreds of blacks and mulattoes to the revolt and had promised emancipation to the slaves.

According to the 1869 census, the male population on the island barely exceeded the female group by 14,159 persons. Some 47 percent of the inhabitants were under 16 years of age. Married persons amounted to 135,397, of which 82,319 were whites, 52,580 were free colored, and 498 were slaves. Of those married, 116,252 were heads of households. The households were classified as 69.4 percent "poor" and 30.6 percent "solvent".[52] Although the terms are not explained by the census, it is significant that the colonial authorities recognized that close to 70 percent of the population was living in poverty. Judging from the wages earned by the 60,000 jornaleros (free laborers), between two and four reales a day, that sector of the working class could classify as wretchedly poor.

The colonial society of the 1860s was generally divided by race, class (often determined by the individual's occupation), and national origin. Much emphasis was also placed on purity of blood (*limpieza de sangre*), education, and political preference. Racial mixtures were distinguished and graded in a hierarchical fashion. According to Julio L. Vizcarrondo, one of Puerto Rico's best known abolitionists, the racial definitions on the island were very complex. There were whites, *"pardos libres"* (free colored) and black slaves. Under the term pardos libres the authorities included mulattoes, *grifos* (children of mulattoes), *mestizos, zambos,* and blacks.[53] White skin was considered a symbol of social superiority, although not all whites were economically well off. Wealth and education could be used by light-skinned Negroes to improve their social status in the society.

The whites were divided between Spaniards born in Spain, called *peninsulares,* creoles (persons born in the colony), and foreigners, who resided on the island. As subjects of the Crown both the peninsulares and the creoles were considered Spaniards, and thus recognized as equals before the law. However, in practice, the creoles were discriminated against and denied employment and economic opportunities enjoyed by the peninsulares. High posts in government, the church, the military, and large-scale commerce were almost always given to the newcomers from Spain. In general, the creoles had relatively little access to the royal officials making those appointments and the colonial authorities distrusted the creoles.

The propaganda circulated before the Lares uprising demonstrates that the creoles complained bitterly against the royal partiality, which gave jobs to Spaniards who they believed were less capable than they. The peninsulares, on the other hand, tended to defend and justify their privileged positions by claiming that the creoles were incapable, lazy, and given to licentious living.[54]

White foreigners were likely to be treated more like Spaniards than like creoles, if they were wealthy, politically conservative, and had the blessings of the Catholic church. The studies by Professors Francisco A. Scarano and Carlos Buitrago have shown that foreigners with wealth and connections could obtain opportunities in the colony that were not possible for the creoles.[55] Many of them, together with peninsulares, became involved in large-scale commerce and in commercial farming. Among the sugar planters of Ponce, Scarano found many foreigners who had amassed much of their wealth at the expense of the creoles. Similar conditions were uncovered by

Prof. Buitrago among the coffee growers of the interior. In both cases, the immigrants often obtained great landed estates by the prevailing method of foreclosing on the farms of individuals in debt to them.

The largest group of the inhabitants lived in the rural area. Urban living was generally preferred by the Spanish merchants and officials, the priest, the military officers, some artisans, and the jornaleros, who after 1850 were forced to establish residence in the towns, where they could be more accessible to the government officials. It was not the practice of the hacendados to live in the urban areas. The creole hacendados were generally not wealthy enough to undertake the added expense of a house in the town when they had to have one in the hacienda. The hacendados of Lares, Camuy, and San Sebastián that we studied were struggling to keep their relatively small haciendas. They, like the men who worked for them, had become dependent on the merchants of the towns for loans, credit, and provisions.

But even in the poorest hacendado's house there was room for numerous relatives and foster children, who like his immediate family, sought his support and protection. Family relationships in this society were dominated by the father, who as head of the house had power over all dependents. Their wives, however, although technically bound by marriage vows of obedience and fidelity, enjoyed some liberties. For example, colonial property laws allowed women to engage in certain economic activities and to keep their own property independently of their husbands. Some women became executors of their husband's wills and other managed their husband's estates after their deaths.[56]

Living conditions for the poor, especially for the jornaleros, deteriorated rapidly after the 1830s, when Governor Miguel López de Baños adopted the policy of regulating the laboring classes. The *Reglamento de Jornaleros* (Worker's Rules and Regulations) issued by the governor stipulated that persons lacking property or resources to meet their needs should seek employment to guarantee their livelihood.[57]

The Reglamento applied to males and females 16 years old and over. They were to register with the municipal board nearest their homes and find employment at once. Those who failed to either register or find employment were admonished by the local authorities. But if they persisted in their attitudes or remained unemployed more than a month, they were forced to work for the state at half pay or, in the worse of cases, sent to jail. Those who could not secure employment in their areas were advised to move to public lots reserved for them in the towns.[58]

The conviction that such coercive tactics led to greater production and complaints from planters that some laborers were escaping the law, led to a refinement of the Reglamento in 1849 by Governor Juan de la Pezuela. He decreed that every jornalero be issued an identifying document, or libreta, and that this passbook be inspected once a month by the local authorities.

As workers continued to escape the regulations by squatting on public lands, or by securing plots from friendly hacendados and/or relatives, the authorities decreed further restrictions, putting an end to the system of *agrego* (a type of sharecropping system). Only laborers employed by the haciendas were permitted to remain on them after June 1850.[59] Hacendados caught giving or leasing land to jornaleros were criticized for encouraging vagrancy and were subject to official reprimand.

Small hacendados and critics of the libreta argued that the system led to many problems which affected the workers as well as the planters. For example, they explained in their letters to the governor that peasant farmers who previously hired out their services part of the year to supplement their incomes would no longer do so for fear of being considered jornaleros and subjected to the libreta system. Others also argued that the jornaleros who worked all year long were unable to plant their food crops, causing their food supply to diminish and their diet to deteriorate.[60]

Thus, by the 1860s, the lives of the jornaleros were generally characterized by hard work, little freedom, low wages, and very little food. Their workday began at dawn and ended at sundown. Their wages, if they were paid in cash, ranged from two reales in the interior of the island, to three or four reales in the coastal haciendas.[61]

Undernourishment among the poor was so common that it was considered to be universal. As one Spanish official reported,

> . . . the wretchedness in which the proletariat lives is such that they are forced to eat what they produce even before it is ready to be harvested.[62]

Hunger, many social critics agreed, was the motive behind the increasing number of food thefts, which in 1864 were responsible for over three hundred court cases.[63]

Low wages and high food prices compounded the problems of the landless worker. For a jornalero earning the equivalent of 10 to 20 centavos a day could not buy such goods as rice, which sold in Lares for 10 centavos a pound, sugar at five centavos a pound, dried codfish, which sold for eight centavos, jerked beef, from Argentina, at seven centavos, lard, from the United States, at 24 centavos, and chocolate, at 20 centavos.[64]

Unable to purchase such foods, the workers lived on starchy roots, a few beans, corn, plantains, and a little coffee they secured from the hacendados. Milk, eggs, and meat were foods they seldom ate. Barefooted, half starved, and overworked, they were easy targets for hookworms, chronic anemia, tuberculosis and other diseases that turned them into pale, thin skeletons before they reached adulthood.[65]

The meager wages they earned were often used to buy clothing, which they could not produce. As a jornalero from Vega Baja reported, the typical wardrobe of a worker consisted of two outfits: one which was being worn, the other which was being washed. Those who had only one outfit, he said, did not go to work on Saturdays so that their wives could wash and iron it in time for them to make a clean appearance at the employer's house on Sundays.[66]

The homes of the jornaleros and poor persons, in general, were described by the same witness as small huts, measuring about five square *varas* (about 13.5 square feet). These were generally raised on poles, were thatched with palm, and served as living room, bedroom, and kitchen. The living room and bedroom floors were made of palm boards and the kitchen had no flooring. Their scant furnishings were a table, made by the worker, a bench or two, and a hammock. "Beds" were simply boards of the same palm which were nailed together by the workers themselves.[67]

According to the 1860 census, only 15,115 individuals of the 138,000 free colored adults had enough property or resources to escape the classification of domestics and jornaleros (see Table III). With the arrival of Spanish military men from Spanish America and with the growing white population after 1815, free colored men were increasingly excluded from the militia units, which had been among the only avenues for social mobility traditionally open to them.

A list of selected occupations for the 1860s indicates that more than half of the peasant farmers, artisans, and proprietors in the colony were members of the free colored population (see Table III). But no person of black lineage was then, or had recently been, judging by their absence among the pensioned civilians, employed by the government in the 1860s.

Of the 39,069 slaves on the island in 1869 about one third (13,446) worked in the fields, alongside 60,000 jornaleros. This fact was emphatically stressed by the island's abolitionists in their proposals for the abolition of slavery. While their arguments were often buttressed by moral precepts, they never lost sight of the economic reality, arguing that slavery was no longer profitable.[68] Although the abolitionists sought the termination of the slave system, they did not always oppose the regulation of the freedmen's labor force. In the abolitionist project presented before the Junta Informativa that met in Spain in 1867, they argued that abolition was desirable "with or without regulation of the freedmen's labor force.[69]

In general, life for the island's poor was far from idyllic in the 1860s. As recognized by the colonial officials, nearly 70 percent of the population lived in poverty even after 50 years of Spanish attempts to develop the island economically. With the growing commercialization of agriculture, the concentration of the arable land in fewer hands, and the coercive labor system, the society had become more stratified than it had been at the beginning of the century. Without industry and other economic avenues, the poor found themselves relegated to a life of misery.

TABLE III
Selected occupations of the inhabitants of Puerto Rico, 1860, by racial groups.*

| | Population Groups | | |
| | Whites | Free Colored | Total |
Occupations			
Peasant farmers	17,395	9,642	27,037
Active military duty, including trained militia	11,133	44	11,177
Retired military personnel	117	12	129
Proprietors	8,855	4,563	13,418
Merchants	3,091	321	3,412
Industrialists (artisans)	891	512	1,403
Manufacturers	26	6	32
Civilian employees	874	0	874
Pensioned civilians	49	0	49
Teachers	454	15	469
Ecclesiastics	159	0	159
Totals	43,044	15,115	58,159

Source: Acosta, "Notas", p. 305.

*This list of occupations does not represent the total number of persons in the labor force that year.

The dilemma of the colonial society did not escape the minds of the various creole liberals, who proposed a better educational system as an alternative for upward social mobility. From the 1840s to the late 1860s there were three governors who agreed with this view and tried to reorganize the primary school system. The problem they faced, however, was that many of the municipalities were too poor to support an extensive school system. Thus, in 1867, the official newspaper, *La Gaceta*, reported the existence of only 252 schools in the entire island. Twelve of them were secondary schools, located in major cities and heads (*cabeceras*) of districts. The rest were primarily rural schools, known as *escuelas incompletas*. These were generally missing something that kept them from operating properly or continuously.[70]

In Lares, in the 1850s, the missing element was the teacher. For two years the municipal board searched for a qualified teacher without success. Of the two who applied, one was disqualified for political reasons and the other for immoral behavior. He was found to be living in sin, with a woman he had not married. For a time the priest assumed the position until the moral offender gave up his concubine and took the job.[71]

The problem in staffing the schools was more often due to the low salary that was offered to the teachers. In Caguas, in 1866, the prevailing salary for a teacher was 180 pesos a year, while the wages paid to the state's executioner was 400 pesos annually.[72] And, as a taxpayer from Caguas commented, the executioner did not work every day of the year.

With such meager educational resources it is no wonder that the majority of the children went unschooled. In 1866, only 4,000 of the 31,000 children of school age (6-12 years of age) were enrolled in school and attending classes.[73]

Illiteracy and widespread ignorance were the rule. According to the official estimates, over 84 percent of the inhabitants were illiterate in 1866. Even those considered literate often knew only how to read or how to write, but not always both. Of the 51,250 persons that possessed such skills, 27,009 were males and 17,719 were females. About 12 percent of the literate persons were from the free colored group.[74]

The educational reforms attempted by the colonial regime were never very successful, in part, because they left the financing of the schools to the wealthier classes. These, as Salvador Brau reported, were not always interested in educating the poorer classes. For, they were convinced that "the jornalero that learns to read and write scorns the hoe."[75] In short, education, like so many other sectors Spain tried to reform, remained an unfulfilled promise which served to inflame the hearts of the Lares rebels.

In conclusion, during the century since O'Reilly's visit, the island underwent many changes that contributed to its delayed insurrectionary spirit and to its continued colonization by Spain long after Spanish America had achieved its independence. New colonial policies adopted by Spain in the late eighteenth century, and during the years of turmoil in Spanish America, led to a transformation of the colony from a neglected, undeveloped and poorly populated possession into a valuable colony.

Sporadic reforms, but particularly those of the Cédula de Gracias, led to a transformation of the colonial economy, to increased productivity, greater trade volume and value, and a population expansion. Temporary political reforms and administrative decentralization improved conditions for some creoles, as they came to be represented in the Spanish government and given a share of participation in the affairs of the colony. When these reforms were no longer possible, there was still enough economic prosperity to smooth the tensions that might arise between the colony and the metropolis. Thus, Spain's apparent commitment to the development of the colony generated an optimism that helped to keep the creoles within the Spanish fold.

Yet, neither the reforms nor the prosperity of the new colonial period lasted. By the 1860s, the colony was once again suffering from many of the maladies encountered a century earlier by O'Reilly. Although government revenues had increased significantly since the 1760s, they were still not enough to cover the expenses of the administration. The expanded bureaucracy and military, coupled with Spain's continous demands for war funds, put a strain on the island's resources. The colonial economy was increasingly decapitalized and its inhabitants were still poor, barefooted and ignorant. Educational facilities were still scarce and land was concentrated in the hands of persons who were not always able to cultivate it. In many ways the problems of the 1860s were more acute, for creole expectations did not coincide with the reality of a society that had become more dependent and more rigidly stratified.

The stagnation of the economy, the unfulfilled political promises, and the growing social tensions required a more flexible and generous policy than the one Spain was capable of granting during this time. Its inability to do so contributed to the conditions that shaped the Lares uprising.

NOTES
1   Quoted from the English translation of O'Reilly's study in R. A. Van Middeldyk, *The History of Puerto Rico from the Spanish Discovery to the American Occupation* (New York: D. Appleton and Co., 1903), pp. 147-148.
2   Ibid.
3   Arturo Morales Carrión, *Puerto Rico and the Non-Hispanic Caribbean* (San Juan: University of Puerto Rico Press, 1971), p. 85.
4   Luis E. González Vales, "Towards a Plantation Society," in Arturo Morales Carrión, Editor, *Puerto Rico: A Political and Cultural History* (New York: W. W. Norton & Co. Inc., 1983), p. 81.
5   John Lynch, *The Spanish-American Revolutions, 1808-1826* (New York: W. W. Norton & Co. Inc., 1973), pp. 1-36.
6   González Vales, Ibid., pp. 86-87; Also Morales Carrión, *Puerto Rico and the Non-Hispanic . . .*, p. 134.
7   Luis E. González Vales, *Alejandro Ramírez y su Tiempo* (Rio Piedras: Editorial Universitaria, Universidad de Puerto Rico, 1978), pp. 9-30; Also González Vales, "Towards a Plantation . . . ," pp. 92-98.
8   Ibid.
9   Ibid.
10 John Lynch, Ibid., p. 2.
11 González Vales, "Towards a Plantation . . . ," pp. 94-95.
12 José Julián Acosta, "Notas" al texto de Fray Iñigo Abbad y Lasierra, *Historia Geográfica, Civil y Natural de la Isla de San Juan Bautista de Puerto Rico*, Annotated Edition (San Juan: Imprenta Acosta, 1866), pp. 349-350.
13 Ibid.
14 The figures for 1830 are cited in Henry K. Carroll, *Report on Porto Rico, with recommendations, 1899* (Treasury Department Doc. 2118) (Washington, D.C.: Government Printing Office, 1900), pp. 119-120 (hereafter cited as Carroll, *Report*); the others are from Acosta, "Notas," p. 329.
15 Harvey S. Perloff, *Puerto Rico's Economic Future: A Study in Planned Development* (Chicago: University of Chicago Press, 1950), p. 18.

16 Prices found in "Diario Económico de la Casa Marquez, No. 4" in *Colección Emiliano Pol*, Archivo General de Puerto Rico (AGPR), Lares 1864-1871, pp. 84-86.

17 González Vales, "Towards a Plantation . . . ," p. 93.

18 Harvey S. Perloff, *Puerto Rico's Economic Future*, p. 14.

19 Acosta, "Notas", p. 324.

20 Ibid., p. 326.

21 See his "Inmigración y estructura de clases: los hacendados de Ponce, 1815-1845," in Francisco A. Scarano, Editor, *Inmigración y Clases Sociales en el Puerto Rico del Siglo XIX* (Rio Piedras: Ediciones Huracán, 1981), pp. 21-66.

22 For a history of the coffee industry in Puerto Rico, see Laird Bergad, "Agrarian History of Puerto Rico, 1870-1930," in *Latin America Research Review*, Vol. XIII, No. 3 (1978), pp. 63-94.

23 Acosta, "Notas", p. 326.

24 Ibid.

25 Perloff, Ibid., pp. 14-15; Acosta, "Notas", p. 328.

26 For a detailed analysis of the economic conditions of the farmers of Lares see Chapter 2 of this work; Also see Laird Bergad's essay, "Hacia El Grito de Lares: Café, Estratificación Social y Conflictos de Clase 1828-1868," in Francisco A. Scarano, Editor, *Inmigración y Clases Sociales . . .*, pp. 143-185; for those of Utuado, see Fernando Picó, S. J., *Amargo Café* (Rio Piedras: Ediciones Huracán, 1981).

27 The fate suffered by the landless coffee workers is best described by Fernando Picó in his essay, "Deshumanización del trabajo, cosificación de la naturaleza: los comienzos del café en el Utuado del siglo xix," in Francisco A. Scarano, *Inmigración y Clases Sociales . . .*, pp. 187-206.

28 Bergad, "Hacia El Grito de Lares . . . ," pp. 155-156; 164.

29 Letter from Manuel María Mangual to Felix María Marchesi, Mayagüez, 2 December 1867, found in the Archivo Municipal de Mayagüez (AMM) Docs. Mun., 1867, Vol. 2.

30 Letter from Mariana Bracetti to Felix María Marchesi, Lares, 12 November 1867 found in AGPR, Fondo De los Gobernadores Españoles de Puerto Rico (FGEPR), Municipios, Lares 1860-1890 Caja 486.

31 Loida Figueroa, *History of Puerto Rico* (New York: Anaya-Las Americas Pub. Co., 1974), pp. 137-139.

32 Julio L. Vizcarrondo, *Elementos de Historia y Geografía de la Isla de Puerto Rico* (San Juan: Imprenta Militar de J. Gonzalez, 1863), p. 38.

33 Loida Figueroa, Ibid., p. 171; Vizcarrondo, Ibid.

34 González Vales, "Towards a Plantation Society," p. 101.

35 Vizcarrondo, Ibid.; Also see, Statement from Luis Muñoz Rivera on the nature of the government, in Carroll, *Report*, p. 15.

36 Salvador Brau, *Historia de Puerto Rico*. Reprint (San Juan: Editorial El Coquí, 1966), pp. 251, 256-258.

37 The gradual displacement of the creoles by incoming Spaniards and foreign immigrants has been well documented in the works we have cited of Fernando Picó, Francisco A. Scarano, and Laird Bergad.

38 Lidio Cruz Monclova, *Historia de Puerto Rico (Siglo XIX)* 2nd. edition (Rio Piedras: Editorial Universitaria, Universidad de Puerto Rico, 1958) I, pp. 124, 477.

39 Acosta, "Notas", p. 386; Salvador Brau, op. cit., p. 249.

40 Brau, op. cit., p. 234.

41 For information on Puerto Rico's contribution to the war in Santo Domingo, see "Expediente Sobre la Expedicion de Santo Domingo: Reintegro de las Cantidades Suplidas por las Cajas de Puerto Rico," in Archivo Nacional de Cuba, Intendencia,

Legajo 829, Exp. 4 (13 folios). A copy of this document can be found in Centro de Investigaciones Históricas, Universidad de Puerto Rico, Colegio de Humanidades.

42   Cruz Monclova, *Historia*, I, pp. 386-389.

43   Ibid.

44   Copy of this letter appears in the Appendix of José Pérez Moris' book, *Historia de la Insurrección de Lares*. 2nd Edition (Rio Piedras: Editorial Edil, Inc., 1975), pp. 280-281.

45   The various taxes are discussed by Vizcarrondo, *Elementos de Historis . . .*, pp. 50, 78; see also Statements by Mr. Andrés Crosas and Mr. Hartmann, in Carroll, *Report*, pp. 366-367, 382.

46   Salvador Brau, *Historia*, pp. 249-250.

47   Pérez Moris, op. cit., pp. 44-49.

48   From census figures cited in Pérez Moris, op. cit., p. 240.

49   Cited in Van Middeldyk, op. cit., p. 215.

50   A cholera epidemic in 1855 killed 31,000 persons, including 5,000 slaves. For more details, see Lidio Cruz Monclova, *Historia*, I, p. 342.

51   Argument presented by Pérez Moris, op. cit., p. 243.

52   Ibid., p. 242.

53   Vizcarrondo, op. cit., p. 52.

54   The judgments about the creoles appear in many official reports sent to the governor during the 1800s.

55   Scarano, op. cit.; Carlos Buitrago Ortiz, *Los orígenes históricos de la sociedad precapitalista en Puerto Rico* (Rio Piedras: Ediciones Huracán, 1976).

56   In the Notarial Records of Camuy, Lares and San Sebastián, I found many cases of women engaging in business matters.

57   For a detailed account of the regulation of labor in Puerto Rico, see Labor Gómez Acevedo, *Organización y Reglamentación del Trabajo en el Puerto Rico del siglo XIX* (San Juan: Instituto de Cultura Puertorriqueña, 1970), pp. 89-90.

58   Ibid.

59   Ibid., pp. 97-98.

60   Ibid., Letters in Appendix II, III and IV, pp. 455-475.

61   Based on statements made by the rebels of Lares to the judge investigating the uprising in 1868.

62   Cited from Darío de Ormachea, "Memoria acerca de la Agricultura, el Comercio y las Rentas Internas de la Isla de Puerto Rico," in Cayetano Coll y Toste, Editor. *Boletín Histórico de Puerto Rico*, 14 Vols., Reprint (Barcelona: Talleres Gráficos de Hija de J. Ferrer y Coll, 1971), II, p. 243.

63   Salvador Brau, "Las Clases Jornaleras de Puerto Rico," presented at the Ateneo Puertorriqueño in 1882 and reprinted with other essays of the same author in *Ensayos: Disquisiciones Sociológicas* (San Juan: Editorial Edil, 1972), p. 46.

64   The prices quoted here were in effect in Lares, see "Diario Económico de la Casa Marquez, No. 4", *Colección Emiliano Pol*, AGPR, Lares 1864-1871.

65   The sickly, pale appearance of the Puerto Rican peasants has been the subject of much iterature. As one example, see Nemesio Canales, "Nuestros Jíbaros," in Servando Montaña (ed.), *Meditaciones Acres* (Rio Piedras, 1974), pp. 128-132.

66   According to a Statement given by the laborer, Severo Tulier of Vega Baja to the U.S. Commissioner, Dr. Henry K. Carroll and which appears in Carroll, *Report*, p. 726.

67   Ibid.

68   Conclusion reached by liberals like José Julián Acosta. For his analysis of the work force and the numbers employed in each sector, see his "Notas", p. 305.

69   Portion of the "Proyecto para la Abolición de la Esclavitud en Puerto Rico" of 1867 which was quoted in Cruz Monclova, *Historia*, I, p. 508.

70   The Lares' school system was discussed by Antonio Rivera, in "Ubicación de un Municipio: Lares," *Historia*, Vol. 5, No. 1, pp. 39-40; the number of schools on the island were quoted in *La Gaceta*, 31 October 1867, p. 3.

71   Antonio Rivera, Ibid.

72   Letter from D. Nicolás Aguayo to Governor Marchesi, Caguas, 31 May 1866 in Labor Gómez Acevedo, *Organización y Reglamentación del Trabajo* . . . , pp. 469-475.

73   Aguayo to Marchesi, Ibid.; Acosta, "Notas", p. 415.

74   Estimates appear in Acosta, "Notas," p. 305; Carroll, *Report*, p. 200.

75   Salvador Brau, "Las Clases Jornaleras . . . ," op. cit., p. 61.

Ramon Emeterio Betances (1827–1898),
leader of the Lares Conspiracy.

Segundo Ruiz Beluis (1829–1867), con-
spirator with Betances.

Ana Maria (Mariana) Bracetti Cuevas
(1825–1903), sewed the revolutionary flag.

II
The Rebels and Their Motives:
Leaders and Followers

According to the official literature, the majority of the rebels charged with taking part in the uprising were ungrateful foreigners, bankrupt industrialists and farmers, desperate jornaleros, vagabonds, criminals and adventurers.[1] But a more dispassionate review of the documents generated by the same official authorities demonstrates that the majority of the insurgents were Puerto Ricans, representatives of the social and racial diversity that existed in the colony.

The Rebels' Birthplace

Based on the information the prisoners provided to the courts, 93 percent of the suspects (see Table IV) were born in Puerto Rico. In other words, of the 551 who were ultimately charged, 512 were known to have been born on the island. Of those born in Puerto Rico, 485 specified the municipality on the island in which they were born (see Table IV).

Nearly 97 percent (468) of the 485 persons born on the island were born in western Puerto Rico. Only 17 were born in the towns of the northeast. The towns of Mayagüez and Pepino accounted for more than one third of the suspected rebels. Although 27 towns contributed their sons to the armed struggle, 10 towns supplied 85 percent of them.

Despite the official propaganda, only 7 percent of the persons suspected, arrested, and/or jailed were foreign-born (see Table V). Among those are included 14 Spaniards, who as Europeans would be considered foreign-born by the rebels.

The evidence that so few foreigners were linked to the uprising proves to be an important fact. For we have been led to believe that what took place in Lares was not only of minor importance, but was the work of a handful of malcontents who were led by ungrateful foreigners.

TABLE IV

Number and percent of suspects, born in Puerto Rico, by municipality

	Number	Percent
Total number of suspects	551	100.0
Born in Puerto Rico	512	93.0
With known place of birth on the island	485	88.0
Place of birth in Puerto Rico not known	27	5.0
Birthplace, by municipality		
Pepino (San Sebastián)	84	15.2
Mayagüez	81	14.7
Lares	48	8.7
Aguadilla	33	6.0
Añasco	33	6.0
San German	30	5.4
Quebradillas	29	5.3
Isabela	28	5.1
Moca	25	4.5
Camuy	20	3.6
Yauco	13	2.4
San Juan	11	2.0
Aguada	10	1.8
Arecibo	8	1.5
Cabo Rojo	6	1.1
Utuado	5	*
Manatí	4	*
Ponce	4	*
Sábana Grande	3	*
Adjuntas	2	*
Trujillo Bajo	2	*
Caguas	1	*
Hatillo	1	*
Guayanilla	1	*
Juana Díaz	1	*
Maricao	1	*
Naguabo	1	*

Sources: For this Table we used the replies given by the rebels to the questions asked by the courts. These appeared throughout the five boxes and the eighteen piezas found in the Archivo General de Puerto Rico (AGPR) concerning the Lares uprising. Also useful was Judge Navascues' Report to Audiencia of 19 February 1869, found in AGPR, FGEPR, *La Revolución de Lares 1868*, Caja 181, Pieza 48.

*Number represents less than one percent.

TABLE V
Number and percent of suspects, born in foreign countries, by country of origin

	Number	Percent
Total number of suspects	551	100.0
Born in countries other than Puerto Rico	39	7.0
Birthplace, by country of origin:		
Spain	14	2.5
Venezuela	9	1.6
Santo Domingo	4	*
Dutch Caribbean	3	*
Africa	3	*
Italy	3	*
France	2	*
Mexico	1	*

Source: This table was compiled from information provided by the rebels themselves. Also useful was Judge Navascues' Report to Audiencia, 19 February 1869, found in AGPR, FGEPR, *La Revolución de Lares 1868*, Caja 181, Pieza 48.

*Number represents less than one percent.

The Rebels' Place of Residence

Information about a suspect's residence was eagerly sought by the courts. Knowledge of a person's residence allowed the judge to gather information about the prisoner's conduct, political inclinations, and, the extent of his economic solvency. Generally, those with little or no property were fined 500 escudos (about 250 pesos), while those of means had their estates attached.

So vital was this information that the residence of only five of all the suspects remained a mystery to the authorities. It should be noted that nearly 60 percent of the prisoners were residents of the municipalities of Lares and Mayagüez.

Generally, all new residents within these municipalities were at once suspected. Movement of residence was cause enough for the authorities to arrest a great number of persons in the municipalities of Pepino, Camuy and San Germán (see Table VI).

TABLE VI

Number and percent of rebels residing in Puerto Rico in 1868, by municipality

	Number	Percent
Total number of suspects	551	100.0
Known person with residences in Puerto Rico	546**	99.0
Places of residences:		
Lares	169	30.6
Mayagüez	160	29.0
Pepino (San Sebastián)	44	7.9
Camuy	35	6.4
San Germán	33	5.9
Quebradillas	14	2.5
Aguadilla	13	2.4
Isabela	13	2.4
Adjuntas	11	2.0
Añasco	10	1.8
San Juan	10	1.8
Utuado	5	*
Ponce	5	*
Yauco	4	*
Manatí	4	*
Hatillo	4	*
Arecibo	3	*
Moca	2	*
Aguada	1	*
Cabo Rojo	1	*
Sábana Grande	1	*
Trujillo Bajo	1	*
Caguas	1	*
Guayanilla	1	*
Juana Díaz	1	*

Source: AGPR, FGEPR, *La Revolución de Lares 1868*, Caja 181, Pieza 48.

*Number represents less than one percent.
**The total includes all except the five whose places of residences were unknown.

General Characteristics of the Rebels

Among the questions most often asked of the rebels by the courts interrogating them were those regarding the type of jobs, trades or professions they engaged in before they were arrested. Generally, they were also asked whether they were able to read and write. Sometimes they were questioned on more personal matters, such as age, color, civil status, and number of children. For the purpose of this section, we only charted those categories that provided sufficiently consistent information.

Occupations, Trades and Professions

The rebels' replies (see Table VII) indicate that nearly 89 percent of the suspects reported the type of jobs, trades or professions they occupied themselves with prior to the uprising. Of those, 34.3 percent were jornaleros, 13 percent were peasant farmers, namely *labradores*, and *pequeños agricultores*,[2] nearly 9 percent were slaves and 6 percent were small, retail merchants, generally known as *pulperos*.

Those who owned land or small businesses represented nearly 25 percent of the suspects and were considered men of certain social standing in the community. Not all, however, were equally well off, since some were small to medium-sized hacendados while others were struggling pulperos and artisans. The one common economic trait they shared was that, whether hacendado or pulpero, they were in debt to the Spanish merchants.

An obvious characteristic of the group sampled is that it represented a wide spectrum of the colonial society's groups and occupations. For example, among the suspects were seven doctors, 189 jornaleros, four tailors, three housewives, three teachers, two priests, five scribes, two bakers, one mayor, one photographer and one musician. The fact that 74 percent of them owned little or no property is another indication that they were representative of the colonial society. According to the official census of 1869, over two thirds of the island's households were considered poor, or headed by persons without means.[3]

Literacy of the Suspects

About 270 of the rebels were interrogated with regard to the extent of their education. Those questioned by the courts were generally asked whether they knew how to "read or write," rather than how many years of school they had completed. Apparently, it was taken for granted that a knowledge of both skills was not necessary to be considered literate for the purpose of the courts. Such questions were asked for functional reasons, such as determining

TABLE VII

Occupations, trades, and professions of the suspects, proprietors included

	Number	Percent
Total number of suspects	551	100.0
Occupation unknown	61	11.1
Known occupation	490	88.9
Occupation distribution:		
Jornaleros	189	34.3
Peasant farmers	74	13.4
Slaves	49	8.9
Merchants	35	6.3
Hacendados	23	4.1
Overseers	15	2.7
Sales clerks	13	2.3
Carpenters	11	2.0
Doctors	7	1.3
Militiamen	7	1.3
Shoemakers	5	*
Comisarios	5	*
Scribes	5	*
Tailors	4	*
Housewives	3	*
Teachers	3	*
Sailors	3	*
Masons	2	*
Bill collectors	2	*
Active militia officers	2	*
Justices of the peace	2	*
Bakers	2	*
Priests	2	*
Notary public	2	*
Cigarmakers	2	*
Printers	2	*
Lawyers	2	*
Unlicensed medical practitioners	2	*
Druggist	1	*
Pharmacy student	1	*
Painter	1	*
Tobacco retailer	1	*

(Continued)

Table VII (Cont.)

	Number	Percent
Candymaker	1	*
Musician	1	*
Photographer	1	*
Hatmaker	1	*
Barber	1	*
Engineer	1	*
Mayor	1	*
Secretary	1	*
Navy officer	1	*
Tax collector	1	*
Retired militia officer	1	*
Constable	1	*
Manager, cockpit	1	*

Sources: Information for this Table was found in the testimonies given by the prisoners, in AGPR, FGEPR, *La Revolución de Lares 1868*, Cajas 176-181, Piezas 1-3, 10-13, 38-44, 46-48. Also useful was Judge Navascués' Report to Audiencia of 19 February 1869, in Ibid., Caja 181, Pieza 48.

*Number represents less than one percent.

in advance whether or not the courts had to provide eye witnesses who would sign on behalf of the illiterates. Hence, ability to write one's name was all that was required in most cases, since the courts had scribes on their premises who could read the prisoner's testimony in case he could not read.

According to the method just described, it appears that 57.4 percent of the 270 to whom the questions were posed knew either how to read, how to write, or both (see Table VIII). In other words, 155 of those questioned were considered literate by the courts. Compared to the total number of suspects, the number that possessed these skills represented about 28 percent. Compared to the rest of the society, these prisoners were proportionally more literate since the official literacy figures of Puerto Rico during the mid-1860s identified over 80 percent of the inhabitants (16 years old and over) illiterate.[4]

TABLE VIII
Number and percent of literate and illiterate suspects

	Number	Percent
Total number of suspects	551	100.0
Status unknown	281	51.0
Illiterate	115	20.9
Literate	155	28.1

Sources: Hundreds of testimonies found in AGPR, FGEPR, *La Revolución de Lares 1868*, Cajas 176-181, Piezas 1-3, 5, 10, 11-13, 38-44, 46-48. In these I found the original transcripts of the testimonies given by the prisoners during the four months the investigation lasted.

Note: Since the 270 interrogated represented 49 percent of the total number of suspects, we felt it would be a good sample of the prisoners exposure to even rudimentary education.

Ages of the Suspects: A Sample

While relatively fewer suspects were questioned about their ages than about personal traits, we found the information available sufficiently valuable to include in this study. The data provided by the 151 suspects, who were interrogated, appears in Table IX. According to this data, it appears that the majority of those interrogated were adults, ranging in ages from 25 to 44 years of age.

Table IX also indicates that as many suspects were in the age group 14 to 24 as there were in the category 35 to 44. Each of these groups accounted for 29 persons.

In sum, while the characteristics of the rebels just outlined do not deny the major role played by the poorer classes in the uprising, they allow one the opportunity to revise the more traditional interpretation advanced by the official Spanish literature. As has been demonstrated, contrary to what the defenders of the Spanish government led the society to believe, the majority of the persons suspected of taking part in the Lares uprising were not foreigners, criminals, nor adventurers, but hard-working Puerto Ricans of the western part of the island. Less than a dozen of them were found to have previous "criminal" records. These generally were for minor offenses, such as not obeying the work regulations or failing to have some official paper on their persons. Although the majority of those arrested were in fact propertyless, about one fourth of them owned land and businesses, paid taxes, contributed to the colonial coffers, built the roads, and supported the local militias.

TABLE IX
A sample of suspects' ages

No. of Persons	Ages	14-16	19-24	25-34	35-44	48-58	60+
1	14						
2	16	3					
3	19						
7	20						
3	21						
3	22						
2	23						
8	24		26				
16	25						
9	26						
6	27						
6	28						
9	29						
15	30						
4	31						
5	32						
6	33						
3	34			79			
4	35						
3	36						
2	37						
4	38						
3	39						
7	40						
2	41						
1	42						
1	43						
2	44				29		
2	48						
5	50						
1	52						
1	55						
1	58					10	
1	60						
2	64						
1	68						4

Sources: AGPR, FGEPR, *La Revolución de Lares 1868*, Caja 181, Pieza 48.

Whether rich or poor, black or white, literate or illiterate, all of them were very much part of the society and not a group of outcasts.

Motives for the Lares Uprising

According to the official correspondence sent by Judge Nicasio de Navascués y Aisa to Governor Julián Juan Pavía, the rebels' motives for revolting against Spain stemmed from their desire to achieve independence, create a republic, and destroy the peninsulares.[5] While in essence this statement recognizes the political goals the rebels were trying to achieve, it does not deal with the economic and social motives the rebels may have had. By focusing on the nationalistic motives, Judge Navascués inadvertently set the stage for the subsequent interpretations of the uprising. Since the nationalistic interpretation is the most accepted by the historiographers of Lares, we have made a great effort to search for motives other than those attributed to nationalism. Our findings are divided into two categories: those stated, or explicit, in the rebel literature and those implicit in the types of problems that many members of the rebel movement were experiencing at the time of the uprising.

The Stated Motives: The Rebel Literature

According to one of the longest proclamations that circulated in Puerto Rico, following the exile of Ramón Emeterio Betances and several other Puerto Rican intellectuals, there were many reasons for their decision to break with Spain. This proclamation, generally attributed to Betances, although it was signed by the *Comité Revolucionario de Puerto Rico* (The Revolutionary Committee of Puerto Rico), was written in an attempt to explain and justify the dissenting actions of those who had been exiled. It stated:

> Puerto Ricans. . . . Our brothers who have left have conspired — and they should conspire — because it is necessary that one day the colonial regime in our island (comes to an) end; because Puerto Rico, like the continent, like Santo Domingo must be free[6]

It should be pointed out that the commitment of the intellectuals implied by this excerpt was only partially true at the time of exile. As Betances himself had the occasion to find out later, only three of those ordered into exile with him were willing to listen to his revolutionary plans. In time, the propaganda that circulated in Puerto Rico after July 1867 together with the myopic policies enforced by Spain antagonized some of the intellectuals and professionals and they joined the rebel movement.

It appears from the literature of the period that although some of the intellectuals declined to join Betances' radical movement they were not satisfied with the conditions of the society.[7] Their complaints against Spain were essentially those summarized by the Proclamation of 1867, which the rebels viewed as reasons for breaking with Spain:

> . . . we are, with the exception of a few dozens, victims of the Spanish colonial system, which since Columbus has been, and will always be, the negation of every right and all justice; the absolute and irresponsible empire of a handful of greedy, inept adventurers; the monopoly of extortionists of all kinds; . . .[8]

The proclamation bitterly complained about the lack of creole participation in the affairs of the colony. Arguing that Spain's preference for the peninsulares would continue so long as the island remained its colony, the proclamation called on the inhabitants to conspire, to end the ties with Spain:

> (We must conspire), because lacking any participation in the affairs (of the colony) we find ourselves crushed under the weight of taxes we do not vote on, and which we (later) see misspent on a small number of inept Spaniards . . . while the native sons of this land, more capable (than they), hold only posts of secondary importance, or jobs not remunerated, . . .[9]

The fact that the colonial regime discriminated against the creoles in the area of government employment is corroborated by the evidence supplied by the rebels about the nature of their jobs at the time of the Lares uprising. For example, from the 490 rebels who reported their occupations, only about 30 of them were employed by the colonial government. These held jobs of secondary importance and most of them did not receive payment for their services.

The regime's preference for peninsular employees weighed heavily on the shoulders of the creole professionals who, deprived of schools and institutions of higher learning in Puerto Rico, were forced to spend their few resources abroad in search of an education, only to return home where they would be deprived of jobs.

There are numerous examples of creoles with fine educations who had a difficult time securing positions in the island's administration. Even those who were fortunate enough to obtain minor positions were not always able to keep them. In most cases personal and political differences with the officials that supervised them led to their dismissal.

Besides the discrimination they suffered in the job market, the rebels also complained of the lack of economic opportunities in the colony. They blamed the colony's economic crisis on Spain's greed and inefficiency. As they stated in the July Proclamation, Madrid not only took one half of the island's revenues, but allowed the rest to be squandered on inept local officials and unnecessary programs. This they viewed as another reason for breaking with Spain:

> We should conspire, because of the five million pesos that we pay in taxes annually, more than one half finds it way to Spain, to never return, under the pretext of surplus, or savings belonging to the (peninsular) employees. The other half is squandered in an unnecessary military force, in a ravenous public treasury, in an immoral administration, in faulty public works, and in a secret police (that spreads terror everywhere).

> We should conspire, because in exchange for these sure calamities and the problems of immorality sown in (our) path by slavery, the economy does not grow in proportion to the efforts spent, but drags on, or stagnates.[10]

While the issue of creole participation in the administration of the colonial government was a cause of concern to the small local elite, the other problems they raised, such as immorality, injustice, corruption, and Spain's greed, were issues the rest of the creoles could identify with and understand. For example, for the average person in Puerto Rico, Spain's greed was visible in the form of increasingly heavy taxes it imposed regardless of the problems afflicting the society. In a society where people scarcely could afford basic necessities, the only things not taxed were dry goods and jewelry.

The fact that the average person was aware of the immorality and corruption prevalent among the Spanish officials is corroborated by the anonymous letters that were sent to the Governor and the Court in Madrid.[11] In one such letter sent to the *Corregidor* of Arecibo, Colonel Manuel de Iturriaga, in 1867, a local resident accused the corregidor of pocketing the money that the municipal corporation had saved for installing gas lights in the plaza and for repairing a bridge.[12] He accused the corregidor of enjoying favors from the Governor and of allowing the public works of the district to decay so that they would have to be rebuilt and he could collect the kickbacks offered by the competing builders.

Often the anonymous letters would be used by the Crown to remove troublesome officials. In this fashion, the Crown maintained an image of impartiality and justice which encouraged the subjects to think that the problem would be solved the minute Spain was notified of its existence. Thus, in 1867, following the exile of a dozen Puerto Ricans by José María Marchesi, a stream of angry letters reached the Spanish officials in Madrid and within a few months the Governor had been removed. The exiles were granted amnesty and provided with safe conduct passes to return to Puerto Rico.[13]

It was apparently this calculated flexibility which worried the leading separatists, for soon after Spain sent a new, much more liberal governor they issued a series of warnings to the populace. In a proclamation, signed by the *Comité del Sur*, the separatists warned against becoming complacent just because Spain had sent them a soft-spoken, new governor, Julián Juan Pavía.[14] The proclamation reminded the reader that the new governor, like his predecessor Marchesi, was just another representative of the colonial government, whose feigned liberalism was, at best, a cover behind which the system hid in order to oppress and exploit the Puerto Ricans. It said:

Puerto Ricans: The Spanish Government is no longer happy with oppressing to exploit (us) . . . these are its rights. General Marchesi, who has left deeds on this soil that demand revenge, is now replaced by a devouring lion wrapped in the cape of a protective father of the poor . . . (acting as) a mediator, . . . to squeeze and exploit (us) later.[15]

Days later, the *Comité Interior de Borinquen* issued a frantic proclamation in which it described the process by which they were deprived of their rights, their property and the opportunity to obtain material goods by the Spaniards. It said:

Puerto Ricans: Look out! We are hitting bottom. . . . The Spanish Government is no longer content with depriving us of all our liberties. . . . The first, and most precious since it is the guarantor of the rest, the right to dispose of the product of one's work . . . has never been ours. Look out! The hand of the government is forever in our pockets. The right to own property (here) is an illusion, for no one can be said to own what another has the right to take away.[16]

The proclamation explained this concept by adding:

The exorbitant contributions, the tax monies (to which we have no access), the scandalous forced loans, the forced subscription for public works, the foreclosures and public auctions that (daily) deprive the unfortunate of his last possession, the well-known robbery of the national lottery, are no longer enough to satisfy Spain's insatiable greed. . . . (Our) hacendados, our merchants, and our farmers are bankrupt, or on the verge of bankruptcy.[17]

In an attempt to turn public opinion against the new governor, the separatists blamed him for the moral destruction of the society, claiming that the new policies he had issued encouraged the populace to relax its moral standards. The same proclamation stated:

License to the husband to leave his wife alone in the evenings, exposed to seductive temptations! License to take, to waste, to lose, to gamble and to steal! . . . Those are the rights that we are given in the name of freedom! Raise your heads high and reject such insults.[18]

Finally, in what appeared to be a last attempt to exhort the creoles to take up arms against Spain, the *Comité Revolucionario de Puerto Rico* appealed to the nationalistic feelings of the people by pointing out the long history of servitude. In an impassioned call to arms, the Comité said:

Friends: four hundred years of oppression and servitude have not abolished our right to be free. That right is part of every man at birth. God grants it to him . . . and without it there is no possible happiness.[19]

The differences that separated the Spaniards from the Puerto Ricans were so profound it added, that they called for a break with Spain. It stated:

Everything separates us from Spain. . . . More than the immensity of the Ocean. . . . The horrors (Spain has perpetrated) on this land: the primitive race, destroyed; the African race, enslaved and sacrificed; and with them, the creole, enslaved, dejected, and scorned, clamors to the Heavens for mercy. . . . The separation (between us) has been made. For us, our beautiful Borinquen; for them, the valleys and the peaks of the Sierra Morena. Long Live Free Puerto Rico! Long Live the People of the Antilles![20]

The revolutionary literature is important if we are to understand the many forces that shaped the Lares revolt. It outlines the many problems afflicting the colonial society under Spain and points to the existence of a creole leadership yearning to take control from Spain. While it would be premature to conclude that the existence of either conflicts, or political leadership was enough to provoke the Lares revolt, it would be naive to dismiss either one as not having, in some way, shaped the event.

The existence of colonial conflicts was not enough to guarantee a revolt any more than the presence of a revolutionary leadership. Both were ultimately influenced by the intransigence of Spain. The way in which those conflicts were mishandled by Spain created the conditions for the emergence of a revolutionary leadership and a political ideology around which to rally the discontented. Once on the scene, the revolutionary leaders provided the ideological justification the followers needed to challenge Spain. Yet even at this time the confrontation could have been avoided by a more receptive Spain. But in choosing the least sensitive approach to the creole problems, Spain left them no choice, but to revolt. As the proclamation of 1867 concluded:

We must conspire, because there is nothing we can expect from Spain nor from its government. Spain cannot give us what (it) does not have. . .[21]

In the following section, we shall demonstrate how the conflicts, articulated by the revolutionary leadership as national problems, affected the local community of Lares. This is not to say, however, that similar problems did not exist elsewhere on the island. Nor is the evidence discussed here an argument in favor of the local scope of the uprising.

The Unstated Motives: The Cases of the Lares Rebels

According to the official report of Judge Nicasio de Navascués y Aisa, there were no causes or motives for the rebellion of Lares other than those stemming from nationalistic sentiment.[22] He insisted on this judgment despite the evidence to the contrary he heard in the rebels' testimonies. To avoid making the same mistake, we have reviewed not only the rebels' testimonies, but various other sources, such as land registries, notary records, tax forms and store records in search of the reasons that led the rebels to revolt. What appears from all these documents is that there were more than one set of motives behind their decision to revolt. Among those reasons, naturally, the rebel leaders claimed "patriotism" as the first cause. Among those who wished to see the island independent was Juan Vicentí, a native of Mayagüez and a member of the secret society, *Capá Prieto*. He testified that he worked with the Lares movement because it "was against Spain."[23] Similarly, Francisco Arroyo Salazar, from Mayagüez, a member of Capá Prieto, who led several dozen men into battle, told Judge Navascués that his motives for attacking Lares had been "patriotism" and the desire to "change the government, [and] to improve the situation of Puerto Rico."[24] Juan de Mata Terreforte, also a native of Mayagüez and the second commander of the rebel troops, told the court that he had "nothing against the Spaniards, but that (he) disagreed with the ideas of the government in power."[25] Francisco Ramírez, a native of Aguada, who became president of the republic the night of 23 September, testified that he joined the rebels because the leaders Manuel Rojas and Baldomero Bauring had persuaded him "of the need to depose the Spanish government and end the oppressive rule."[26]

Although we have no reason to doubt the sincerity of these replies, they are not enough to explain the uprising. They make no mention of the many conflicts that separated the Spaniards from the creoles. Nor do they explain why the revolutionary leadership arrested the Spanish merchants of Lares and put their account books to the torch as soon as they occupied the town.

The first possible explanation was given by Governor Pavía on 8 October. In his message to the inhabitants of Puerto Rico, he stated that the motives for the revolt were linked to the critical economic conditions the island had been experiencing since the previous year.[27] He traced the economic problems to the natural disasters suffered by the island that year and the revolt to a "small group of bankrupt creoles and ungrateful foreigners."[28]

In his report to the government in Madrid, Pavía blamed the rebellion on persons contrary to Spain. He added that the "tax increase and other contributions have come at a bad time, as they are to be collected precisely during the time that the drought has left the jornaleros jobless."[29]

Governor Pavía's assessment of the motives for the uprising makes sense in light of the correspondence that was exchanged between the colonial treasury and several ayuntamientos (municipal corporations) during the late 1860s. For example, on 5 June 1867 the Junta of Mayagüez, in response to a questionnaire from the colonial treasury, stated that the projected taxes needed for administrating the municipality during the fiscal year 1867-68 was 90,999 escudos and 291 milésimas.[30] This sum, the Junta explained, did not include the "extraordinary expenses" which probably would amount to an additional 32,434 escudos and 832 milésimas, and which would have to be collected from the non-agricultural sectors. The Junta explained that despite their efforts to adjust the new taxes there would be a deficit of 70,129 escudos and 503 milésimas for the incoming year.

Mayagüez would find no relief in the colonial treasury. The reply sent by the acting intendant, Juan M. Ortiz, argued that Mayagüez' population had doubled in the last 30 years, thus, it followed that its production should have also doubled and more taxes should be paid to the colonial treasury.[31] According to the formula he devised, the minimum value of taxable production per inhabitant should not be less than 100 escudos per year, rather than the 50 escudos estimated by the production figures submitted by the municipal Junta.[32]

Hoping to make an example of Mayagüez, the intendant rejected Mayagüez' figures, arguing that about three fourths of the (municipal) production was not being taxed. After a long speech in which he warned the mayagüezanos against the immorality of depriving the government of its due revenues, the intendant asked to be paid in advance 25 percent of the taxes owed for the fiscal year 1867-68. The government coffers were so depleted that they could not wait until the end of the fiscal year, when they should have been paid in full.

This insensitivity at a time of economic troubles and rising taxes alienated some of the creoles and pushed them to revolt against the increasingly oppressive system. The rising taxes and the severe measures used by the collectors were, according to the United States Consul in Puerto Rico, Alexander Jourdan, the main reasons for the revolt.[33] A similar judgment was made a year after the uprising by the colonial delegate, Don Luis Padial, before the Spanish Cortes. Alluding to the unjust taxes imposed on Puerto Rico during the two previous years, Padial said: "the many requests and oppressive actions by which the treasury demanded the impossible, produced a profound discontent and a general alarm among the proprietors that culminated in the desperate attack of Lares."[34]

The deteriorating economic conditions of Mayagüez were further compounded by the destruction of the crops caused by the hurricane of October and the earthquakes of November 1867. According to a letter from the syndic of Mayagüez, Manuel María Mangual, a member of the revolutionary group, the two disasters set the production in his district back two years.[35] He described the economy of the island in general, and Mayagüez in particular, as suffering from a "profound malaise" for several years. He added that the disasters of late had made the conditions critical, requiring that the government intervene to bail out the district. He described the sugar haciendas, the most valuable to the economy, as barely able to cover their losses that year. He stressed that, among the poor, conditions were extremely difficult. The flooding of the rivers and the winds of the past hurricanes had destroyed hundreds of dwellings, leaving thousands of unfortunate souls homeless. Hundreds of persons had drowned and animals and crops needed for feeding the populace had been destroyed. After a detailed description of the suffering of his district, Sr. Mangual requested, on behalf of the taxpayers of Mayagüez, exemption from all colonial taxes for the following two years.

The reaction to Sr. Mangual's letter by the treasury was not unpredictable. The intendant asked the Corregidor of Mayagüez, Colonel Antonio de Balboa, to submit his views on the nature of the district's economy. On 17 January 1868 Colonel Balboa submitted a report, which included some charts on the productivity of the region's major crops and industries.[36]

In essence, Colonel Balboa's assessment agreed with those of the Junta and Sr. Mangual that the district was in economic trouble. What varied, however, were the Colonel's interpretations as to the causes of the economic plight. Unlike Sr. Mangual, Colonel Balboa attributed the economic problems to the declining productivity and the increasing consumption of imported goods. The first, he attributed to the poorer classes' unwillingness to work and the latter to the creoles tendency to consume more than they produced.[37]

He blamed the laborers' unwillingness to work on the climate and the types of foods they consumed, adding that an abundance of wild fruits and vegetables coupled by the workers' "tendency to steal" made it possible for the poorer classes to survive without having to work.

He added that the practice of increasing consumption had led to a shortage of coin which, in turn, had caused the bankruptcy of many farmers and industrialists of the district. Declining productivity, he argued, had forced Mayagüez to import such staples as rice, grains, codfish, and salted beef, causing an unfavorable trade balance and the economic plight of the region.[38]

Whether Colonel Balboa's report was instrumental in the trade policy that followed is hard to say. But by September 1868 the colonial government was considering abolishing the imports tax exemption. Alexander Jourdan alerted his government:

> I have no faith in the stability of the actual exemption from import duties. There is now a deficit in the revenues of the customs since January 5th (compared with the same period last year) of 600,000 pesos, and to cover it the local government has found no other expedient way but to double the rate of taxes on agriculture, commerce and industry, making thus illusory . . . the benefit intended by the exemption from duties declared on the articles of general consumption and creating a considerable dissatisfaction and fermentation through the whole island. I would not be surprised if the Governor of Puerto Rico would advocate, before long, the former import duties.[39]

The island was faced by economic problems the government was incapable of solving and, in fact aggravated by raising taxes. The cry against "unjust taxes," according to the slave Polinario, was the main argument he heard from the rebels on the way to Lares.[40]

Yet, rising taxes were not the only problems strangling the farmers of western Puerto Rico. For a number of years before the rebellion erupted, the coffee farmers of Lares had become dependent on the Spanish merchants for cash loans to finance production, imported goods on credit, and access to the coffee market. The excessive interest rates charged on the loans, the expense of imported goods taken on credit and the low price paid to the farmers for their crops led to mounting debts they could seldom pay. When this happened, the merchants foreclosed on the debt and often deprived the farmers of their land. In times of economic troubles as in 1867 their problems were further compounded by the drought, hurricane and rising taxes.

To illustrate this point, let us review the conditions that bound the pulperos and farmers to the merchants of Lares. The geographic area that became the municipality of Lares in 1832 had been until then a *barrio* (ward) of Pepino (San Sebastián).[41] Neglect by that municipal government and the growth of the population in Lares caused the largest taxpayers of the area, led by Juan Francisco de Sotomayor, to petition the colonial governor to make Lares an independent municipality in 1827.[42] After the customary review, to ascertain the facts that Lares had the needed requirements for incorporation, the municipality was born under the government of the *Junta de Visita* (an appointed, rather than elected, governing board) composed of Don Pedro Jiménez, Don Francisco de Sotomayor, Don José de Xara, Don Antonio Toledo, Don Juan Díaz, Don Juan Martín Soto, Don Joaquín del Rosario Méndez, and Don Antonio del Río.[43]

For the purposes of administration the new municipality was divided into 12 barrios, one of which would be called Lares, like the town.[44] According to the first report submitted by the Junta of Lares, the population of the new town in 1832 was 1,676 persons, of which 500 males, ages 16-60 had been enlisted in the urban militia.[45] By 1842 the population had increased to 3,411 persons, among whom resided 28 slaves.[46] Twelve of the 28 slaves belonged to one landowner, named Juan Bautista Fremaint, a Frenchman who settled in Lares in 1838.[47] According to one historian, the first settlers of the municipality came from the nearby municipalities but the latter immigrants came from Spanish America, France, the Balearic Islands, and the province of Catalonia, Spain.[48]

From the very beginning the economy of Lares was based on agriculture, particularly on the production of coffee for export, and commerce.[49] At first the production of the export crop was in the hands of the creole families of the area, but as the immigrant population grew the land was gradually concentrated in fewer hands, particularly in those with greater capital to acquire large farms. Twenty years later, most of these farmers would find themselves defending their land from the latest arrivals, the merchants from the coastal towns and the commercial agents of European houses who settled in Lares.[50]

For example, between 1844 and 1863 at least four large commercial establishments had taken root in Lares. The first, known as Casa Marquez, was started by Don Juan Marquez in the mid 1840s, shortly after he arrived in Lares as an employee of Doña María de Soto.[51] Don Juan, according to one historian, put his salary to good use investing it in a small store and lending it to others at a profit.[52] As a member of the colonial elite, Don Juan knew how to read and write, talents which by 1844 landed him a post as alderman (*regidor*) of Lares, which, in turn, led him to the position of acting mayor of the municipality.[53] Apparently, the combination of talent, prestige, and opportunity, opened the road for the great fortune that was acquired by the Marquez family. A few years after he settled in Lares Don Juan sent for his four brothers and together they founded the powerful Casa Marquez y Compañía.[54]

According to the Casa Marquez' records, in 1863 the firm was in the hands of Don Juan's younger brothers, Don Antonio, Don Baltazar, and Don Miguel.[55] That same year these three brothers reorganized the business, investing into it a total of 38,149 pesos. Within two years their capital had more than doubled.

Between 1867 and 1868 the Marquez brothers expanded the business allowing a nephew, Don Miguel Marquez, Jr., and two non-family members, Don Pedro Mayol and Don Francisco Frontera, to invest in Casa Marquez.[56] They brought to the firm an additional 35,589 pesos, making the total worth of Casa Marquez in 1868 about 86,123 pesos. In one year's time the investors were happy to learn that their capital had grown by 42,165 pesos, making the total sum an astronomical 128,288 pesos, of which 31,483 pesos were owed them, or in accounts receivable.[57]

While Casa Marquez was the largest commercial firm in Lares it was not the only one. Among some of the others were: Francisco Ferret y Hermanos (Hnos.), a branch of the powerful firm from Aguadilla, Amell, Juliá y Co., Juan Alcover y Co., Cristobal Ferrer y Co., Frutos Caloca y Co., and Vivó, Méndez y Co.[58] It appears that most of these were started by ex-employees of Casa Marquez and business associates of Amell, Juliá y Co. For example, the founder of Juan Alcover y Co., Juan Alcover, a native of Mallorca, was employed by Casa Marquez in 1863 helping to carry out their liquidation sale. From there Juan Alcover and a member of the Marquez family, Don Ramón, went to found Juan Alcover y Co. Don Cristobal Ferrer, a native of Catalonia (Spain), also worked for Casa Marquez before starting his own business. Francisco Ferret started out as a representative of Amell, Juliá y Co. and by the 1860s had become a powerful rival to Casa Marquez.[59]

As pioneers in the Lares' trade, the Marquez brothers seemed to have set the standards for doing business in the area since most of the houses that came later operated in the same fashion.[60] Generally, they served several purposes, as they became importers of foods, manufactured goods, farm implements and textiles and exporters of coffee and other minor crops. But, according to the Casa Marquez' books, the merchants' greatest function was to extend cash loans and credit to the farmers in the area.

The transactions recorded by the commercial houses during the years 1863 to 1868 indicate that the farmers were in constant need of cash and credit. Those who were advanced both credit and loans were to pay back partly in cash and the rest in crops, preferably in coffee. The debt, accumulated by the extension of credit, was paid in installments and no additional interest was apparently charged. But the cash borrowed by the farmers had to be paid within one or two years at the rate of 12 to 18 percent yearly. In most cases, the farmer's future crop was used as guarantee and when that was not enough to cover the debt, the farm was placed as collateral.[61]

The merchants' financial advantage often led to the ruin of many farmers since, in addition to their ability to control the prices of exports and imports, they had the right to foreclose on any debtor whenever they pleased. The prompt payment of the interest on the debt did not always guarantee that the farm would not be attached for foreclosure.[62]

For example, among those caught in the merchants debt-foreclosure cycle were several farmers from Lares, who later joined the rebel movement that culminated in the Lares uprising. The best known among them was Manuel Rojas, president of the revolutionary cell, *Centro Bravo No. 2*, and the military leader who guided the rebel troops into battle in September 1868. The history of Rojas' indebtedness appears to have begun in 1862, when he purchased a 569 cuerda *estancia* (name given to small and medium-sized farms), partly planted in coffee and food crops, with a house and some farm tools, from the commercial establishment of Aguadilla, Amell, Juliá y Co.[63] Not having the full 56,000 escudos (23,000 pesos) the sellers required, Rojas bought the farm on credit and borrowed from the same firm 3,800 pesos to finance his farming operations. Four years later (1866) he declared to the notary, Evaristo Vélez, that his debts with Francisco Ferret amounted to 28,510 escudos, despite the fact that he had been paying regularly in coffee, cotton, and cash. He promised to pay all the cash loans made by Ferret y Hnos. at the rate of "12 percent yearly."

By May 1868 Rojas had bought and mortgaged several estancias in (barrios Mirasol, Pezuela) Lares, which pushed him further into debt with Francisco Ferret y Hnos.[64] According to the notarial notice of 7 May 1868, Rojas consolidated all his debts with that firm by mortgaging all he owned for the sum of 51,378 escudos.[65] On that same day, Rojas ceded to the notary, Evaristo Vélez, a farm of 15 cuerdas he owned in barrio Mirasol, Lares in payment for the 1,862 escudos he owed Vélez.[66] On 26 May 1868 Rojas asked the commercial establishment of Vivó, Méndez y Co. for a loan of 7,903 escudos to carry him over until January even though he already owed that firm over 3,000 escudos.[67] Vivó, Méndez y Co. agreed to the loan requesting, in turn, to be paid in "good quality coffee and all other production not already claimed by Ferret y Hnos."[68] A 12 percent interest rate was stipulated on the cash they gave Rojas. On 12 April 1869 Ferret y Hnos. foreclosed on Rojas, leaving him with an unmortgaged plot of 11 cuerdas in barrio Mirasol, which Rojas sold seven days later for 400 escudos.[69]

But the story of Rojas economic woes was not unique. Of the 30 known members of the rebel cell Centro Bravo No. 2, we identified 12 who were in desperate economic conditions, due to debts. Among them was Francisco Ramírez, the vice-president of the revolutionary cell, and later president of the republican government set up in Lares. According to the notarial records, Ramírez had to cede his store (pulpería) in barrio Bartolo (Lares) to the firm of Francisco Ferret y Hnos, in March 1869.[70] In addition to that business, Ramírez had to give Ferret y Hnos. a horse, a cow and all the accounts receivables in his favor, totalling about 830 escudos.

His brother Manuel Ramírez, also a member of the rebel cell Centro Bravo No. 2, who became Minister of State of the republican government, had also come into hard times. His records show that by 1862 Manuel had to mortgage one of his two estancias to satisfy his creditors Amell, Juliá y Co.[71] His debts to Amell, Juliá y Co. were related to the pulpería he owned in Lares. As guarantee for the 10,656 escudos Manuel owed, the firm demanded the estancia of 67 cuerdas he had in barrios Buenos Aires and Latorre (Lares).[72]

In 1862, Manuel Ramírez' debt had climbed to 12,350 escudos (6,175 pesos) when Amell, Juliá y Co. sold it to Cristobal Ferrer y Co.[73] To pay

Cristobal Ferrer, Manuel was forced to borrow from the commercial house of Juan Alcover y Co. By 1866 Both Ferrer and Alcover demanded their money and Manuel was forced to sell the remaining estancia of 80 cuerdas, with houses, and coffee trees, he owned in barrios Buenos Aires and Latorre (Lares). The sale of that farm brought him about 20,000 escudos, barely enough to pay his creditors.[74] Between January 1867 and February 1868, Manuel Ramírez bought and lost to his creditors, Vivó, Méndez y Co., a small farm of 18 cuerdas.[75] In May 1868 he also lost his pulpería. At the time of his involvement in the Lares revolt, Manuel was employed for someone else, as caretaker of a cockpit.[76]

Andrés Pol, the Treasurer of the rebel cell, Centro Bravo No. 2, and one of the generals who under Rojas attacked Pepino, was also experiencing financial difficulties. According to the notarial records, Pol had to give three farms he owned in barrio Mirasol (Lares) to his creditor, Francisco Ferret y Hnos. The farms, partly planted in coffee, plantains, and other food crops, and totaling about 60 cuerdas, were given by Pol to Ferret y Hnos. to satisfy a debt of 8,000 escudos.[77] In June 1867 Pol stated before the notary of San Sebastián that he was giving the pulpería he owned in barrio Mirasol to Juan Alcover y Co., as guarantee for the 12,073 escudos he owed that firm.[78] He explained to the notary that he failed to make his February 1867 payment and had been warned by Alcover that failure to pay in the future would lead him (Alcover) to foreclose. To make the payment easier, Alcover agreed to divide the total sum owed into payments of 1,200 escudos, to be received every January, until the debt was cancelled. There is no mention whether Pol paid anything to Alcover that day or whether he was able to meet the payments as promised. However, the classification of *vago* (a person without known employment) he received by the authorities during his term of imprisonment,[79] indicates that by 1868 he had lost all he had to his creditors. Another detail that makes us suspect his economic ruin was that in August 1868 he sold what appeared to be his only four cuerdas of land in barrio Mirasol (Lares) to pay another creditor, Juan Vivó.[80]

His brother, Bernabé Pol, member of the rebel cell Centro Bravo No. 2, general under Rojas, and named Secretary of the republican government,[81] also owed more than he could pay. According to the notarial records for 1866, Bernabé purchased from José Ramón Hernández an estancia of 60 cuerdas, with a house, and partly planted in coffee and plantains, in barrio Bartolo (Lares) for the total sum of 9,215 escudos.[82] The same records show that he did not have the money for the first downpayment and simply borrowed 1,240 escudos from Francisco Ferret y Hnos., promising to pay it back, with interest (1,654 escudos), a year later, in January 1867.[83] To Hernández, Bernabé promised to give another payment of 1,000 escudos in February 1868.[84] What happened to Bernabé Pol between February 1866 and May 1868 was not uncommon for the farmers of Lares. Between 1866 and 1867 Bernabé borrowed money from Juan Alcover y Co. to finance his operations and when that merchant demanded payment Bernabé borrowed from Francisco Ferret y Hnos. In conclusion, by February 1868, Bernabé found himself owing Francisco Ferret y Hnos. 3,358 escudos, despite the fact that he had been paying "in coffee," and owing the balance of 7,900 escudos for the estancia to José Ramón Hernández.[85] Hernández, himself under pressure from his creditor, Manuel Muñoz, demanded payment from Bernabé in February 1868. Unable to pay, and incapable of borrowing any more from Ferret, Bernabé took a loan of 700 escudos from Frutos Caloca y Co.[86] While we have no record of Bernabé losing his estancia, we think it was a matter of time before Ferret or Hernández foreclosed on him for lack of payment.

Another well-known Lares rebel, suffering under the tight economic grip of the merchants, was Joaquín Parrilla. Parrilla, who became the celebrated patriot of the separatists for giving up his life instead of surrendering to the Spanish troops, was the secret society's "brother instructor." He was charged, by the authorities investigating the Lares uprising, with having led a number of Rojas' troops into Pepino. According to the notary records of Lares and San Sebastián, Parrilla owned a pulpería and seven acres of land in barrio Mirasol (Lares).[87] The pulpería, according to the same records, was kept afloat by the repeated loans and credit Parrilla secured from Francisco Ferret y Hnos. In December 1865, Parrilla declared before the notary public that he owed Ferret 5,549 escudos and promised to pay them, plus interest, by December 1866.[88] But Parrilla, like many of the farmers and pulperos of the area, failed to meet his payments. On 6 May 1868, Parrilla lost everything he owed to Francisco Ferret y Hnos.

Although we have stressed the cases of the rebels of Lares there is also similar evidence for the rebels of Camuy, San Sebastián, and Mayagüez. In all of these municipalities the farmers and pulperos were caught in a strangling economic web from which few saw a way to escape.

From the viewpoint of some rebels from the poorer classes, the issue of economic survival was also linked to the overthrow of the Spanish government. According to their testimonies, they joined the cause of freedom because they had been promised food and work once the Spaniards were removed from governing the island. For example, Bonifacio Aguería, a resident of the municipality of Hatillo, stated that he had joined the Camuy rebel society, *Lanzador del Norte*, because being in great need he had been assured by Manuel María González that once the new government took command he (Aguería) would be given work and a chance to earn a living for himself and his family.[89]

Similarly, Juan Pedro Arocho, a native of barrio Puertos (Camuy), testified that he had joined Lanzador del Norte because he had been told by Manuel María González that there were two well-stocked warehouses in Mayagüez that would supply those in need enlisted in the cause of liberty.

He added that he had also been told that the entire population was involved in the plot and those who did not cooperate would be ill viewed by the patriots.[90]

Economic reasons, however, were not the only antagonisms between the powerful Spaniards and the downwardly mobile creoles. Racism also became a weapon to keep the creoles out of government and the Spaniards in control. The case of Pascasio Lamourt and Bernabé Pol are examples that illustrate the point.

On 15 January 1863, the new mayor of Pepino, Don José G. Coca, complained to the governor that among the staff of the *alcaldía* there was a mulatto acting as auxiliary scribe. After explaining that such a person could only cause distaste among those who visited his office, the mayor requested that the governor terminate Lamourt's post.

The case dragged while the governor requested a report on the conduct and abilities of Lamourt. And on 26 July the mayor once again requested the removal of this scribe. Despite the positive report provided by the municipal commission and Lamourt's refusal to resign, the governor sided with the mayor and fired Lamourt on 12 August 1863.[91] Lamourt was among the rebels who stormed Lares in 1868.

The case of Bernabé Pol was somewhat similar although it took place in Lares. In 1858, Pol sent a letter to the governor requesting official permission to continue the civil service career he had entered by becoming secretary of the municipal alcaldía. As was the custom, the governor notified the mayor of the municipality and asked for a full report on Pol's conduct and background. The reply sent by Mayor Enrique O'Neill put an end to the aspirations of Pol. For although the mayor found no obvious fault with the young man, nor in his work as secretary of the alcaldía, he chose not to recommend him because of the color of his skin.[92] Pol too joined the rebel cause and the morning of 24 September was named secretary of the republican government established in Lares.

It has been shown that the rebels who stormed Lares had more than one reason for wanting to break with Spain. While many of the rebels were undergoing severe economic hardships, others suffered discrimination, enslavement, and semi-enslavement under the Spanish colonial system. Social and racial barriers kept the majority of the creoles from obtaining their goals. The physical presence of Spaniards in government jobs, commercial establishments, and even in the church were more than symbolic reminders of what the creoles had to endure under Spain. Yet the mere existence of these problems is not enough to explain the revolt. It shall be demonstrated that the political ideology and the revolutionary path marked by the revolutionary leaders were just as important as the prevailing antagonisms in motivating the Lares revolt.

NOTES

1   Message from Governor Julián J. Pavía, "A los Habitantes de Puerto Rico," given in San Juan, 8 October 1868, in AGPR, *Audiencia Territorial, Tribunal Pleno*, Caja 7, Pieza 1, pp. 51-52.

2   While we found no official definition of a small farmer, the reality they presented was not very different from that of the labradores. Thus, we decided to join the two groups under one and the same category.

3   Excerpts of this Census are found in Pérez Moris, *Historia de la Insurrección de Lares*, 2nd. Edition (Rio Piedras: Editorial Edil, Inc., 1975), p. 242.

4   José Julián Acosta, "Notas" al texto de Fray Inigo Abbad y Lasierra, *Historia Geográfica, Civil y Natural de la Isla de San Juan Bautist de Puerto Rico*, Annotated Edition (San Juan: Imprenta Acosta, 1866), p. 305.

5   The statement by Judge Navascués y Aisa was made in the *Informe Final* he submitted to the Governor of Puerto Rico on 19 December 1868, in AGPR, FGEPR, *La Revolución de Lares 1868*, Caja 181, Pieza 48.

6   The proclamation dated 16 July 1867 was published on 1 September 1867 in New York City and signed by The Revolutionary Committee. Copies of this and other proclamations are found in AGPR, FGEPR, *La Revolución de Lares 1868*, Caja 179, Pieza 41; and in Pérez Moris, *Historia de la Insurrección de Lares*, pp. 292-302. Hereafter all references to this document will be cited as *Proclamation 16 July 1867*. All excerpts were translated by the author of this work.

7   For a sample of the issues raised by some of the men who turned down Betances' offer to declare war against Spain, see the writings of José Julían Acosta, 1865-1870; those of Francisco Mariano Quiñones, 1866, 1888; Eugenio María de Hostos, Julián Blanco Sosa and others.

8   *Proclamation 16 July 1867*.

9   Ibid.

10 *Proclamation 16 July 1867*.

11 Letter from Governor José L. Sanz to the Overseas Minister about the rampant corruption of the civil servants in Puerto Rico, 11 June 1869, a copy of which appears in AGPR, *Obras Públicas* (Asuntos Varios), Caja 144, Legajo 181.

12 A copy of this letter was published by José Pérez Moris in *Historia de la Insurrección de Lares*, pp. 280-81.

13 Except for Ramón E. Betances and Segundo Ruiz Belvis, who were the only ones who refused to obey the Governor's order. For details, see in Lidio Cruz Monclova, *Historia de Puerto Rico (Siglo XIX)*, 2nd. Edition (Rio Piedras: Editorial Universitaria, Universidad de Puerto Rico, 1958) I, pp. 439-40.

14 Copy in José Pérez Moris, *Historia de la Insurrección de Lares*, p. 288.

15 Ibid.

16 Copy of this proclamation appears in Pérez Moris, Ibid., pp. 300-301.

17 Ibid.

18 *Proclama del Comité Interior de Borinquen* in Pérez Moris, Ibid.

19 Copy in Pérez Moris, Ibid., pp. 299-300.

20 Pérez Moris, Ibid.

21 *Proclamation 16 July 1867*.

22 Nicasio de Navascués y Aisa to Audiencia, 24 September 1868, in AGPR, *Audiencia Territorial, Tribunal Pleno*, Caja 7, Pieza 1, p. 13.

23 Juan Vicentí was a pulpero, 25 years old, at the time of his involvement in the Lares revolt. For the biographical data, see "Estado demonstrativo de los procesados . . ." in A.H.N., Madrid, *Ultramar, Gob. de P.R.*, Legajo 5111, Exp. 34, Doc. 2; also in AGPR, FGEPR, *La Revolución de Lares 1868*, Caja 181, Piezas 47, 48. For

Vicentí's testimony, see *Boletín de Historia Puertorriqueña*, Vol. II, No. 5 (Abril 1850), pp. 130-160; Ibid., No. 6 (Mayo 1950), pp. 162-192; Ibid., No. 7 (Junio 1950), pp. 192-206.

24 Francisco Arroyo Salazar was a 24 year old hacendado from Mayagüez who was the "hermano instructor" of *Capá Prieto*. The same sources as for Vicentí in the preceeding footnote. Arroyo's testimony is found in *Boletín de Historia Puertorriqueña*, Vol. II, No. 5, p. 160.

25 Ibid., p. 164.

26 The testimony quoted is from *Boletín de Historia Puertorriqueña*, Vol. II, No. 7 (Junio 1950), p. 196.

27 *Circular del Gobernador Julián Juan Pavía*, "A los Habitantes de Puerto Rico," 8 October 1868. Copies in AGPR, FGEPR, *La Revolución de Lares 1868*, Caja 176, Pieza 3. Also in José Pérez Moris, *Historia de la Insurrección de Lares*, pp. 305-307.

28 Ibid., p. 306.

29 In AGPR, FGEPR, *La Revolución de Lares 1868*, Caja 176, Pieza 3. Also in José Pérez Moris, Ibid., pp. 309-314.

30 See "Acta de Ayuntamiento (de Mayagüez)" 5 June 1867 in AMM, *Documentos Municipales* (Docs. Mun.) (Bound Documents), 1867, Vol. 2.

31 Letter from Juan M. Ortiz to the Junta of Mayagüez, 19 October 1867, in AMM, Docs. Mun., 1868, Vol. I.

32 Juan M. Ortiz to the Junta of Mayagüez, Ibid.

33 Alexander Jourdan to the United States Secretary of State, William H. Seward, 4 October 1868, in *United States Consular Despatches*, Vol. 2, Despatch 91.

34 Copy of the document appears in Coll y Toste, Editor. *Boletín Histórico de Puerto Rico*, 14 Vols., Reprint (Barcelona: Talleres Gráficos de Hija de J. Ferrer y Coll, 1971), IV, pp. 33-72.

35 Letter from Manuel María Mangual to the Intendant of Puerto Rico, 2 December 1867, in AMM, Docs. Mun., 1867, Vol. 2.

36 Report of Colonel Antonio de Balboa to the Intendant, 17 January 1868. Copy in AMM, Docs. Mun., 1869, Vol. I.

37 Colonel Balboa to the Intendant, Ibid.

38 Colonel Balboa to the Intendant, Ibid.

39 Jourdan to Secretary Seward, *United States Consular Desptaches*, Vol. 2, Despatch No. 90, (21 September 1868).

40 The slave Polinario belonged to the rebel leader José Antonio Muse (alias Garzón), who, in turn, was the step-son of Matías Brugman. See testimony of 25 September 1868, Mayagüez, which appears in AGPR, FGEPR, *La Revolución de Lares 1868*, Caja 177, Pieza 11.

41 For a detailed history of this municipality, see Generoso Morales Muñoz, *Fundación del pueblo de Lares* (San Juan: Imprenta Venezuela, 1946), pp. 157-58.

42 *Enciclopedia de Clásicos de Puerto Rico*, 6 Vols. (San Juan: Ediciones Latinoamericanas, 1971), VI, pp. 304-305.

43 Antonio Rivera, "Ubicación de un Municipio: Lares," *Historia*, Vol. 5, No. 1, pp. 3-61.

44 Ibid., p. 34.

45 Ibid., p. 10.

46 Ibid., p. 17.

47 Ibid., p. 16.

48 Ibid., pp. 15-16.

49 Ibid., p. 33.

50   The best known commercial house in the northwest quadrant of Puerto Rico in the 1830s was Amell, Juliá y Compañía, located in the port town of Aguadilla. The house was founded by the Amell brothers, from the island of Menorca, and the Juliá brothers, from the province of Catalonia, Spain. For that house's history, see in AGPR, *Protocolos Notariales* (Prot. Not.) *San Sebastián* 1865, Caja 1469, f. 429.

51   AGPR, *Prot. Not. Lares* 1846, Caja 1430, f. 24. According to Estela Cifre de Loubriel, Don Juan Marquez came to Puerto Rico from the Balearic Islands in 1840, *La formación del pueblo puertorriqueño: La contribución de los catalanes, baleáricos, y valencianos* (San Juan: Instituto de Cultura Puertorriqueña, 1975), p. 369.

52   Ricardo Camuñas Madera, "Lares a mediados del siglo 19: Antecedentes económicos a la revolución de 1868," *Una Historia de Servicio* (66th Anniversary Commemorative Edition). (Inter American University of Puerto Rico, 1978), p. 77.

53   AGPR, Prot. Not., *Lares*, 1844, Caja 1430, r. 25.

54   The four Marquez brothers who followed Don Juan to Lares were: Don Francisco, Don Antonio, Don Miguel, and Don Baltazar. Except for Don Miguel, who did not join the other brothers in business until 1863, the rest were well established in Lares by 1851. For details on the transactions of the Casa Marquez prior to 1863, see in AGPR, *Prot. Not. Aguadilla 1851*, Caja 1284, ff. 315-316; Ibid., Caja 1285, ff. 125-26; and in AGPR, FGEPR, Caja 485, Entry 273. For the transactions of this house after 1863, see in AGPR, *Colección Emiliano Pol*, "Diario de la Casa Marquez, No. 4," (Lares 1864-1871).

55   AGPR, "Libro de Inventario de la Casa Marquez y Co.," *Colección Emiliano Pol*, Lares 1864-1871.

56   Ibid.

57   Ibid.

58   AGPR, *Colección Emiliano Pol*, Lares 1864-1872 "Diarios" Correspondientes a las Casas Francisco Ferret y Hnos., Juan Alcover y Co., Cristobal Ferrer y Co., Frutos Caloca y Co.

59   Ibid.

60   See in AGPR, "Libro de Inventario de la Casa Marquez y Co.," Lares 1864-1871; "Diario No. I de la Casa Mercantil Amador Fronteras," Lares 1869-1878.

61   See documents signed by Manuel Rojas and Francisco Ferret in AGPR, *Prot. Not., Lares 1862-1869*.

62   The process by which the merchants deprived farmers of their lands has also been studied by Fernando Picó, Laird Bergad, Vivian Carro Figueroa, and Carlos Buitrago Ortiz.

63   All the above information was taken from the notarial record of 16 May 1866 which appears in AGPR, *Prot. Not., Lares 1868*, Caja 1426, f. 191.

64   AGPR, *Prot. Not., Lares 1868*, Caja 1426, f. 191.

65   AGPR, *Prot. Not., Aguadilla 1868*, Caja 1239, fols. 191-199.

66   AGPR, *Prot. Not., Lares 1867*, Caja 1424.

67   AGPR, *Prot. Not., Lares 1868*, Caja 1426, f. 239.

68   AGPR, *Prot. Not., Lares 1869*, Caja 1426.

69   AGPR, *Prot. Not., Lares 1869*, Caja 1426, p. 329.

70   For the role Ramírez played in the revolutionary cell and the revolt that took place in Lares, see AGPR, FGEPR, *La Revolución de Lares 1868* Caja 181, Piezas 47, 48. For the information about his properties and his business deals with Francisco Ferret y Hnos., see in AGPR, *Prot. Not., Lares 1868*, Caja 1426, fols. 7, 222, 407.

71   Manuel Ramírez' participation in the conspiracy and revolt in Ibid., "Estado demonstrativo de los procesados . . ."; his debts to Amell, Juliá y Co. appear in Ibid., *Prot. Not., San Sebastián 1861*, Caja 1465, f. 557.

72   Ibid.

73   Ibid., *Prot. Not., San Sebastián 1862*, Caja 1466, f. 605.

74   According to the notarial records for 1864, Ramírez owed Ferrer 4,851 pesos and Alcover 2,832 pesos, or a total of 7,683 pesos (15,366 escudos), a bit less than what he obtained for the sale of his estancia of 80 cuerdas. For all this information, see in AGPR, *Prot. Not., Lares 1866*, Caja 1424.

75   Ibid., *Prot. Not., Lares 1868*, Caja 1426.

76   In the official papers of the Lares insurrection, Manuel Ramírez was classified as *vago* (a man without recognized employment) which in the government's view made him a pariah. Ramírez' classification and official charges are found in AGPR, FGEPR, *La Revolución de Lares 1868*, Caja 181, Piezas 47, 48; also in a document that appears in *Boletín de Historia Puertorriqueña*, Vol. II, No. 2 (Enero 1950), p. 66.

77   AGPR, *Prot. Not., San Sebastián 1866*, Caja 1470, f. 225.

78   Ibid., *Prot. Not., Lares 1867*, Caja 1424, f. 230.

79   See copy of the document that appears in *Boletín de Historia Puertorriqueña*, Vol. II, No. 2 (Enero 1950), p. 66.

80   Ibid., *Prot. Not., Lares 1869*, Caja 1427, f. 468.

81   AGPR, FGEPR, *La Revolución de Lares 1868*, Caja 177, Pieza 5; also in Ibid., Caja 181, Piezas 47, 48.

82   AGPR, *Prot. Not., Lares 1866*, Caja 1424, f. 39.

83   Ibid., *Prot. Not., Lares 1867*, Caja 1427, f. 153.

84   Ibid., *Prot. Not., Lares 1866*, Ibid.

85   Ibid., *Prot. Not., Lares 1868*, Caja 1426, f. 59.

86   Ibid.

87   AGPR, *Prot. Not., San Sebastián 1865*, Caja 1469, f. 565; Ibid., *Lares 1867*, Caja 1424, f. 163.

88   Ibid., *San Sebastián 1865*, Ibid.

89   Bonifacio Aguería had been born in Asturias (Spain), lived in barrio Pajuil (Hatillo), and was charged with having taken part in the conspiracy to overthrow the Spanish government. In AGPR, FGEPR, *La Revolución de Lares 1868*, "Estado demostrativo de los procesados . . . ," Caja 181, Pieza 47, 48. The quotation is from his testimony of 6 December 1868 given in Arecibo to Judge Navascués. A copy of this testimony appears in *Boletín de Historia Puertorriqueña*, Vol. II, No. 5 (Abril 1950), p. 140. The fact that Aguería was in an economic squeeze is born out by the notarial records of Camuy.

90   According to the testimony of Juan Pedro Arocho, of 6 December 1868, Arecibo, which appears in *Boletín de Historia Puertorriqueña*, Vol. II, No. 5 (Abril 1950), p. 140.

91   See the *expediente* of Lamourt which starts with a copy of the "Acta Original del Pepino" of 7 May 1862, in AGPR, FGEPR, *Municipios*, Pepino 1863, Caja 582.

92   In the *expediente* of Bernabé Pol appears a copy of his birth record which places him among the mulattos of the municipality even though his father was a Mallorquín. For more details, see his petition in AGPR, FGEPR, *Municipios*, Lares 1830-1850, Caja 485.

III
The Conspiracy Leading
to El Grito de Lares

By 1865, when the new liberal government took the helm in Madrid, Puerto Rico had nearly lost its hope of ever getting the promised "special laws." The island had been denied representation in the Spanish Cortes since 1837, when the last Spanish liberal regime refused to admit its delegates and those of Cuba. Since that time, Spain had promised to govern both islands by a new set of special laws that would befit their "special circumstances."[1] Nothing came of the promise and Puerto Rico became subjected to 28 years of despotic rule, under conservative military generals. On 21 December 1865, however, the new liberal regime that took over the government in Madrid issued a decree requesting that Cuba and Puerto Rico send delegates to the metropolitan capital. The colonies were instructed as well to hold elections and to choose delegates who could form part of a *Junta Informativa* that was to review the pressing problems of both colonies.[2]

The news of colonial participation in the new Junta stirred the Puerto Ricans into action. Creoles of liberal and separatist persuasions put aside their differences and joined forces against the Spanish conservatives, in an effort to win the elections.[3] Well-known separatists such as Ramón E. Betances and Segundo Ruiz Belvis were among those who participated in the elections. In fact, Betances was among the nominees for the district of Mayagüez until he ceded his place on the ballot to his dear friend, Segundo Ruiz Belvis, who won that district seat on the colonial commission.[4]

The Puerto Rican commission that was chosen to represent the island in Spain was composed of eight members, six elected (three conservatives, two liberals, one radical), and two conservatives appointed by the Governor.[5] In the end, only one of the five conservative members of the commission made it to Spain. The rest took so long to get ready for the trip that the Junta opened without them and Governor Marchesi declared their posts vacant.[6] With only one conservative left in the group, the other commissioners (Ruiz Belvis, Acosta, and Francisco M. Quiñones) made plans to push for the abolition of slavery, economic reforms, and political decentralization.

Their plans, however, almost miscarried since by the time the Junta convened, 30 October 1866, the government that had invited them had fallen

to a less receptive group headed by General Narvaez.[7] As in 1837, there
was some talk about sending the delegates back to the colonies without
a hearing.[8]

Despite the turn of events, the Puerto Rican delegates, José Julián Acosta,
Francisco Mariano Quiñoñes, Manuel Zeno Correa, and Segundo Ruiz Belvis
were allowed to present their reports and make some recommendations. In
essence, what they asked for resembled the reforms granted at the beginning
of the century by King Ferdinand.

Politically, they subscribed to the report of the Cuban delegate, José
Morales Lemus, who demanded decentralization of the colonial government,
more creole participation in the administration of the colony, and equitable
representation. They demanded also the right to vote for any male of 25
years of age who paid the state 25 pesos a year in taxes.[9] Neither the Cubans
nor the Puerto Rican commissioners lobbied for universal suffrage.

The economic problems of the colonies were left to a sub-commission
headed by the Spanish economist, Luis María Pastor. The demands agreed to
by José Julián Acosta and the Cuban, Pedro Sotolongo, included reciprocal
free trade between Spain and the two colonies, free registration for all foreign
ships, and a direct tax, not to exceed 6 percent of the net product. The
latter was meant as a replacement of the long list of indirect taxes that were
charged by colonial customs.[10] Their goal was to improve trade relations,
increase production and equalize the tax burden, which at that time weighed
more heavily on the shoulders of the farmers.

On the "social question," a euphemism for the problem of slavery, Ruiz
Belvis, aided by Acosta and Quiñones, drafted a report (*Proyecto para la
abolición de la esclavitud en Puerto Rico*) calling for the immediate abolition
of slavery.[11] Such a demand created a stir in Spain and generated a great deal
of protest among the slavers in Puerto Rico.

The Junta's work came to its end on 27 April 1867 without securing any
of the reforms requested by Puerto Rico. The delegates were sent home with
only a vague promise that the "special laws" would soon follow. Instead, the
Madrid government chose to increase the tax burden,[12] while on the island
the abolitionist delegates faced harassment from the slavers and government
officials.

A special target of harassment was Segundo Ruiz Belvis. Days after he
returned from Spain, the military commander of Mayagüez, Antonio de
Balboa, insulted Ruiz Belvis and tried to run him over with his horse. The
incident provoked a rivalry between the two men, as Ruiz Belvis, a man
known for his stern character, dragged Balboa off the horse and beat him
with the whip he used for the animal.[13] Less than a year later Ruiz Belvis was
accused of attacking the government and expelled from Puerto Rico.

The opportunity to rid the island of known and suspected dissenters
presented itself in June 1867, when the artillery troops stationed in San Juan

revolted. Although the mutiny was an internal protest against a recent military decree which excluded colonial troops from the benefits of a two year reduction in their service,[14] the Governor blamed it on the Liberals and expelled them from the colony.[15]

Those ordered to leave the island were: Ramón E. Betances, Segundo Ruiz Belvis, Calixto Romero Togores, Pedro Gerónimo Goico, Julián Blanco Sosa, José Celis Aguilera, Rufino Goenaga, Vicente María Quiñones (mistaken for his cousin Francisco Mariano Quiñones), Carlos Elio Lacroix, Luis de Leiras and Felix del Monte.[16] Except for the Cuban Luis de Leiras, all the exiled were Puerto Ricans. All, except Betances and Ruiz Belvis, obeyed the Governor's order by presenting themselves before the Queen. To the governor's displeasure the exiled were allowed to return home soon after they had told their stories. One commissioner who escaped deportation was José Julián Acosta. Unlike the other commissioners, Acosta had stayed in Spain and thus escaped the governor's wrath.

A number of factors contributed to the governor's decision to expel those men. For two years he had been hearing rumors that a revolution was in the making to liberate Cuba and Puerto Rico. At least that is what he said to the Governor of Cuba in his letter of 13 December 1866.[17] He confided that news from the Spanish Minister in Washington had led him to believe that "a vast conspiracy is ready to break to proclaim the independence of these two islands." He added, that the Minister's report "corroborates my own suspicions that the conspirators . . . are getting organized under the direction of the revolutionary junta in New York." To demonstrate his diligence, he explained how "for a while now I have been watching some persons very closely, among whom are some from that island (Cuba). He mentioned Doctor Luis de Leiras as one such Cuban whose "sudden and frequent trips from one municipality to another on this island make me suspect him." He speculated that Puerto Rico "may be the place where the rebels may want to strike first to distract Spain from Cuba." And added that he had "discovered about 3,000 men ready to revolt in 1865, under the pretext of gathering an army to support Benito Juarez of Mexico."[18] He undoubtedly exaggerated the figures to get the Cuban Governor's attention and the additional military troops he was requesting.

He justified his request by stating that he feared U.S. intervention since the rebels could probably enlist many "disbanded United States soldiers, who, accustomed to military life, are eager to return to the jobs they do best, especially if they are offered good rewards."[19]

He emphasized the point that with the meager resources at hand he could only handle a local revolt if it did not have outside support. Although he did not elaborate on the counter-insurgency measures he would take in case of a local revolt, it is now known that he counted on the military plan presented to him by Lieutenant Colonel Sabino Gamir y Maladeñ on 9 August 1866.[20]

The Gamir Plan

Gamir's counter offensive plan (Plan Ofensivo Conveniente para Combatir la Insurrección) seemed to have been drafted with Marchesi's fears in mind. It stated that its function was to combat any local insurrection that might erupt with the United States aid. It added that the abolitionist propaganda could stir the free blacks and the slaves to revolt if the abolitionists were protected by the United States.

The Gamir Plan provided the blueprint the governor needed to combat the expected revolt. The first part predicted which sectors of the society and which geographical regions would most likely rebel. The second part offered several recommendations on how to deal with each of these. According to the Plan, the first sector to watch out for was the Spanish military troops stationed in San Juan. It reasoned that these men "could be lured into revolting if they are led to believe that things in Spain have taken a turn for the worse."[21] This was an obvious reference to the unstable political situation in Spain, which had led to two military takeovers between 1865 and 1866. It was also a reminder that in recent years, the Spanish troops in San Juan had demonstrated their support for the Madrid government of their preference by staging mutinies in the barracks.[22] In 1866 there was the additional worry that the soldiers had not been paid their salaries for months. Governor Marchesi voiced this concern to the Governor of Cuba when he stated:

> I lack even the necessary funds to pay the salaries of the soldiers and other public officials. There appears to be some grumbling, and although I do not yet have cause enough to doubt their loyalty, I am concerned that our enemies may take advantage of our troubles to stir the masses.[23]

The second sector Gamir feared was the creoles of those areas "closest to large slave population centers, but far from the military bases." Based on this formula, the Plan rejected the likelihood of armed revolt in the urban centers of Mayagüez, Arecibo, Aguadilla, Caguas and Ponce since these, as the *cabeceras* of their districts, were well protected by military garrisons. These were also disqualified because they were "well connected to San Juan by military roads, which makes the movement of troops and equipment a relatively easy task."[24]

Dismissing other areas for other reasons, the Plan focused on those most likely to rise, namely the western part of Puerto Rico. Within that region the municipalities of Utuado, Lares and Pepino (San Sebastián) were feared because "the great distance that separates these from San Juan, as well as their proximity to Santo Domingo (Dominican Republic), their access to the port of Guánica, their greater wealth, and the bad disposition of its inhabitants" make it the most likely region to revolt.

To counter either a creole or a military uprising the Plan offered two basic strategies. The first, aimed at the military troops stationed in San Juan, recommended using the urban militia of the capital to fight back. But if the revolt originated with the creoles, the Governor was to appeal to the loyalty of the military troops to put down the revolt.

If the insurrection broke out in the western region, as was expected, the Governor was to send military detachments to surround the major ports (Aguadilla, Mayagüez, Arecibo, Guánica and Ponce) which would block the rebels' exit to the sea.[25] Time would prove the accuracy of the Gamir Plan, for it was in the western region where armed resistance started. It was also right about the rebels need of those ports when the revolution failed.

The Lares Conspiracy Takes Hold

By ordering the exile of the island's intellectual leaders, Governor Marchesi thought he could buy some time for his administration and prevent the uprising he feared. But he did not count on Betances and Ruiz Belvis disobeying his orders. Instead of going to Spain as the governor requested, they fled to the Dominican Republic. They reached that island, according to Betances, in July 1867, a month or so after they had been deported.[26]

The tragicomic aspect of their escape was described by Betances in a letter to his friend Eladio Ayala. About the Spanish coast guard, he said: "as soon as it was known that Dottoir Betanzo (sic) had left the island in a poor boat, good canoes and the best horses were sent to those places where he was most likely to disembark, to bring him back to the capital comfortably."[27] He added that the feigned stupidity of a peasant, who guided them through the southern ports, saved them from the authorities. "In Guayama," he said, "we were recognized, despite the care of the *jíbaro* accompanying us." He was in charge of answering all questions, and when the curious asked: 'Where are you from?' He would answer: 'Who, we?' 'We came from up there; have gone down there, and are now going up there again.' Betances, obviously amused, added that in making these replies, "he would keep the most serious face."[28]

To his brother, Adolfo, Betances described the escape a bit differently.[29] He described the place they landed in Santo Domingo as "the most barren land there ever was; a sandy, rocky surface covered with scrub brush and Carib mosquitos." The mosquitos, he joked, were probably "the same that chased the Spanish conquerors from Guánica during the time of the conquest." The journey had been "unbearable, the drinking water was hot, the crackers turned moldy, the cheese became rancid, and I became delirious with fever." He spent the nights "hallucinating, crouched down in the boat, wet to the bone." Upon landing at *La Montalva*, "I threw a blanket (on the beach) and laid there to rest, but the mosquitos forced me to get up; to eat moldy crackers and cheese and drink coffee." The coffee, he had mentioned to Ruiz Belvis, reminded him of "the absent patria."[30]

But despite these problems, neither Betances nor Ruiz Belvis remained idle in exile. From Santo Domingo, with the aid of friends like Gregorio Luperón, they reached New York City in August. While in that city, they learned through the newspaper *The New York Herald* that Governor Marchesi had put out an order for their arrest, charging them with sedition.[31] They answered the charge in a letter to the editor of *The New York Herald*, after they identified themselves as the men sought by the Governor of Puerto Rico. They explained the circumstances that led them to flee the island in the following manner:

> The Government of (Puerto Rico), acting arbitrarily, as is its custom, without a due process, decreed the expulsion of several (persons) of good social standing, among which we are included . . . asking these for (their) word of honor that they would go to the Overseas Minister in Madrid. We have refused to pledge our word for several reasons that in time will be known, and because it would be a waste of time, effort, and money to rely on the good faith of such a government.

In New York City, the two men contacted the *Sociedad Republicana de Cuba y Puerto Rico*. Through that society and a friend from Mayagüez, Doctor José Francisco Basora, who had co-founded the Republican Society, they met a number of Spanish American exiles, particularly Cubans, who were interested in the liberation of both Caribbean islands. They met the Cuban rebel Manuel María Macías and the Chilean Benjamín Vicuña Mackenna.[32] Vicuña Mackenna, on a secret mission in the United States, apparently offered hope if not aid to the Society to start a war against Spain. Vicuña let it be known that Chile, then embroiled in war with Spain, could use a war in either island to divert Spain's attention. For this, naturally, the Chilean government would be willing to help support the Society's rebel cause.[33]

Judging from the events that followed, it seems that the trip to New York convinced Betances and Ruiz Belvis that it was time to depose the Spanish Government. A month later (September 1867), they were back in Santo Domingo making plans for the revolution of Puerto Rico. Between September and October of that year they traveled back and forth between Santo Domingo and Saint Thomas to talk to their compatriots on their way to or from Spain. At the Saint Thomas port, they presented their revolutionary plan to Carlos Elio Lacroix, Julián Blanco Sosa, Rufino Geonaga, José Celis Aguilera and others.[34]

Their reactions, however, were short of what Betances had hoped for. In a letter to Basora, in January 1868, Betances summarized their views as follows: "(Calixto) Romero, like most of our compatriots, had never, I think, considered the question of rights and has (thus) settled for saving his own person. (Julián) Blanco, after offering to work for our cause, and not to ever step foot in Spain, has lied to us. Ever since he saw the path open by Romero, he has run to kneel at the feet of the Queen."[35] José Julián Acosta, he said, turned him down, for reasons Betances interpreted to be born out of fear. He portrayed Acosta as a man more concerned about his personal interests than about the homeland. He described Román Baldorioty de Castro as too tolerant of others, adding, "Castro (sic) . . . does not want (us) to write (to him), nor mention his name, until we have obtained I don't know how many millions. He has the excuse of his family . . . and excuses for the rest."[36]

Betances reserved his praise for those who helped him to found the *Comité Revolucionario de Puerto Rico*. They were: José Celis Aguilera, Carlos Elio Lacroix, Mariano Ruiz (brother of Segundo Ruiz Belvis), José Francisco Basora (in New York), and a priest from the Dominican Republic, Father Fernando Meriño.[37] The *Comité Revolucionario* chose Segundo Ruiz Belvis to gather support for the Puerto Rican rebel cause in Latin America.

Ruiz Belvis' mission was shortlived since he was found dead in his hotel four days after he landed in Valparaíso, Chile. The death notice published in *El Mercurio*, a Valparaíso newspaper, simply said that Ruiz Belvis, "already sick when he reached this port, was found dead in the hotel Aubry, on 3 November."[38] The tragic death of his friend made Betances suspect that he could have been murdered.[39] Recent studies however, indicate that he died from a bladder obstruction.

Without Ruiz Belvis and no one else to replace him the support they were hoping for from South America was lost to them. Undaunted, Betances pushed on, publishing in Saint Thomas two proclamations which urged the Puerto Ricans to break with Spain. In the first proclamation Betances declared Ruiz Belvis a martyr of the cause of independence[40] and in the second he outlined the conditions under which Puerto Rico could continue to be ruled by Spain.[41] The conditions, known as *Los Diez Mandamientos de Hombres Libres* (The Ten Commandments of Free Men), were: (1) abolition of slavery; (2) the right to fix taxes; (3) freedom of worship; (4) freedom of speech; (5) freedom of the press; (6) freedom to trade; (7) freedom of assembly; (8) the right to carry arms; (9) inviolability of the citizen; (10) the right to elect their own public officials. If Spain grants us these liberties, Betances concluded, we will remain loyal to her. But convinced that Spain would never change her ways, he added, "if Spain is willing to grant us these rights . . . , she can (also) send us a governor made of straw who we will hang and burn on Easter Week, in commemoration of all the Judases that until today have sold us out."[42]

Betances' activities caused the Governor of Puerto Rico to seek his expulsion from Saint Thomas and Santo Domingo. In a letter to his Venezuelan friend Pedro Lovera, Betances said: "I will remain here (Santo Domingo) because the doors in Saint Thomas have been closed to me. I heard from some friends that the Danish police is looking for me, since the Danish government made some arrangements with that of Spain."[43]

In Santo Domingo too he had antagonized the government by supporting the Dominican rebels José María Cabral and Gregorio Luperón, who were struggling to depose Buenaventura Báez' regime. His house had become a meeting place for Puerto Rican and Dominican separatists, and this unsettled President Báez. At the end of April (1868) the Dominican police issued an order for Betances' arrest, which he escaped by seeking asylum in the United States Embassy.[44]

Despite the continuous harassment, Betances and three other members of the Comité Revolucionario drafted a temporary constitution. This document authorized them to organize and supervise all revolutionary activity in Puerto Rico. The constitution, adopted in Santo Domingo on 10 January 1868, had as its slogan Simón Bolivar's saying: *"unión! unión! o la anarquía os devorará,"* (Unite, Unite, or Anarchy will devour us.)[45] The members who drafted the constitution and assumed the leadership of the rebel movement were: Ramón E. Betances, Carlos Elio Lacroix, Mariano Ruiz, and the Dominican, Ramón Mella.

As drafted the constitution gave the directors powers to appoint *delegates* and *agents* as their representatives. These would, in turn, travel to and from Puerto Rico, to organize and supervise the formation of secret societies, or rebel cells. The societies known as *juntas* and *legaciones*, were to rally people to the revolutionary cause. The agents were also expected to collect funds from the rebel cells' members to help finance the revolution.[46]

According to the organizational structure they devised, the parent revolutionary cell was in Santo Domingo, where Betances and the directors of the Comité Revolucionario resided. The Comité, through its agents, would be responsible to the juntas, or rebel cells established in the island's urban centers, which, in turn, would be responsible to the legaciones, or rural cells established in the countryside.

The parent cell in Santo Domingo was presided by Betances, while the juntas in Puerto Rico chose their leaders from among their members. The standard requirement was that the president be a member of the Comité Revolucionario. A president of a junta who also belonged to the parent cell in Santo Domingo was known as a *delegate*. His duties, according to the constitution, were to coordinate activities between the juntas and the legaciones, to distribute the proclamations sent by the Comité Revolucionario, to collect funds from the members of the rebel cells, and take them or send them to Betánces in Santo Domingo, to distribute weapons sent by the Comité, and to submit a monthly report about the progress of the rebel cells.

The rebel cells or secret societies on the island had a set hierarchy. Each had a president, a board composed of several aides to the president, and the general members, known as *hermanos*.[47] Each board, in turn, had a president, a treasurer, a secretary, an agent of *relaciones exteriores*, or liaison between the various societies, and the *hermano instructor* who taught the members of the cell the secret language of the organization, trained them in secret codes by which to recognize other members, and trained them in the use of weapons, when these became available. He, like the president and the agent, was among the most important members of the organization.

Each society was free to set up its own rules and regulations regarding its internal operation. For example, the *reglamento*[48] of the Camuy rebel cell, *Lanzador del Norte* stipulated that the president of their society should be a man respected by the other members and that he should have recruited at least 30 members by the time he assumed his post. The agents (also known as *priores*) did not always have to be members of the Comité Revolucionario to be accepted as aides to the president of the cell. The agents' place and duties within the organization were determined by their work, their commitment to the rebel cause, and their ability to recruit at least 10 new members per agent. In Camuy, it was the agents, not the president, who decided who could or could not join their society. Generally, they excluded all Spaniards and anyone whose livelihood depended on them. The agents were also responsible for the physical and financial security of all the society's members. In case of arrest, death, or other problems the families of the rebel members were to be cared for by the organization.[49]

The duties of the average member, or *hermano*, were: to be ready to fight whenever their leaders called; to serve as guard at the home of the president of the society, where documents and funds were kept; to be prepared to alert the others in case of attack. Given the restrictions imposed by the government on traveling, any member who secured a travel pass was required to alert the organization, and be ready to act as a courier.[50]

All members, regardless of class, or position within the organization, were required to take the following oath:

I swear by God and by my honor to be faithful to this society, to obey all its precepts, to keep its existence secret, and to cooperate with money and my personal services to its support, being ready at all times to do as I am told or may destiny take me.[51]

The presidents of the secret societies took an additional oath devised by the Comité Revolucionario which read:

I swear by my honor to carry out faithfully the obligations of the post conferred upon me by the Comité Revolucionario de Puerto Rico, to submit to the Constitution, and to defend it against attack, and to work toward the independence of Puerto Rico as long as I live. Should I break my oath, I deserve to be despised by all honest men.[52]

Part of the brother instructor's duty was to insure the secrecy of the activities of the rebel cell by teaching each and every member a secret greeting that would allow one member to recognize another without risking exposure. Each member, according to the documents from the Camuy society was taught to ask and reply the following:

Q. "What do you do?"
A. "Useful things."
Q. "Give me a letter."
A. "L" (for Liberty), or
   "M" (for *Muerte* or Death).

The men asking these questions were, at the same time, extending their hands for the secret handshake. This included raising their right hand to the level of their right ear and then tapping each other's wrist very lightly. If the two members meeting were the presidents of their societies, they would generally identify themselves by their pseudonyms, which often were names of Taino Indian chiefs.[53]

When communicating through the mails, the members were instructed to use the secret alphabet provided by the Comité Revolucionario. The alphabet simply substituted the letters of the Spanish alphabet for signs and numbers. For example, letter *A* was substituted by a dash (−); *B* was replaced by number one (1); *C* was represented by the equal sign (=); small *d* was substituted by the plus sign (+); *f* by the letter (c); *j* by number five (5); and so on.[54] The writer never signed his name. Instead he used a pseudonym by which he was known among the rebels. For example, if the writer was Matías Brugman, he would sign under the pseudonyms of *Mississippi* and *Capá*; Manuel Rojas would sign as *Tacoma*; Manuel Cebollero as *Rápido*; Eusebio Ibarra as *Esperanza*.[55]

The agents, or aides to the president of the society screened future members for good conduct. No member could be given to drinking, gambling, or any other activity that blemished his reputation and risked endangering the organization.[56] The agents also kept the rebels throughout the island informed of the new developments in Cuba and in Spain. That information was often vital to the societies' plans. For example, they reasoned that if the dissenting Liberals succeeded in taking over the Spanish government again, they would be unlikely to send troops against them. But even if the Liberals sent troops, it would be a lot harder for Spain to squelch the revolution if both Cuba and Puerto Rico revolted at the same time.[57]

The rebel cells also prescribed severe punishments for anyone who disobeyed the rules and endangered the organization in any way.[58]

In sum, by January 1868 the rebel leadership, although in exile, had managed to provide the discontented in Puerto Rico with a plan, an organization, and the appropriate channels through which they could work to depose the oppressive government. It was the responsibility of the rebels on the island, however, to organize the rebel cells, collect funds and send them to Betances to purchase weapons and finance an invading expedition. The number of secret societies that were ultimately organized has been a subject for speculation. The consensus, however, seems to be that there were a lot more than the four exposed by the Spanish authorities during the investigation of 1868-69. The first to speculate on this matter was the judge investigating the uprising. In his report to the *Audiencia* of Puerto Rico, he said that he had enough information to believe that there were additional cells working for the independence of Puerto Rico.[59] He speculated that if there was a *Centro Bravo No. 2* there had to be *Centro Bravo No. 1*, and if there was a *Lanzador del Norte* there had to be a *Lanzador del Sur*, and so on. Since we have found no evidence to substantiate his claims we shall limit our discussion to those societies that were in operation at the time of the Lares uprising.

The Rebel Cells Prepare for the Uprising

According to the Betances' documents published by Bonafoux only two of the societies that participated in the uprising had been officially recognized by the Comité Revolucionario by February 1868. These were *Capá Prieto No. 1*, in Mayagüez, and *Centro Bravo No. 2*, in Lares. Both of them were accepted by the Comité on the same day, 24 February 1868.[60] In other words, the two oldest societies only came into existence seven months before the rebels took to the streets chanting "long live free Puerto Rico."

In February, the Comité also met to name three agents, or delegates. Those named were: José Celis Aguilera,[61] assigned the northeastern area around the capital, San Juan; Carlos Elio Lacroix,[62] the southern area of Ponce; and Juan Chavarri,[63] to organize Mayagüez.

At the end of February 1868 the Lares and Mayagüez societies had chosen their juntas and were presumably working toward the goal of independence. In Lares, the junta of Centro Bravo was composed of Manuel Rojas, President; Francisco Ramírez, Vice-President; Andrés Pol, Treasurer; Manuel Ramírez, Secretary; Joaquín Parrilla, brother instructor; Clemente Millán, agent of relaciones exteriores and two alternates: Mariana Bracetti and Miguel Pol.[64]

Among the members of Centro Bravo, not included in the policymaking process, but considered important to the society, were: Aurelio Méndez, merchant, money lender, and Justice of the Peace in Lares; Cristino Zeno Correa, Méndez' secretary; Bernardo Cuinlan, the scribe to the *cabildo* of Lares; and the *hacendados* Dionisio Colón, Pedro Pablo González, and the brothers Gabino and Leopoldo Plumey.[65]

In Mayagüez, Capá Prieto had its headquarters in barrio Furnias, in the home of its president, Matías Brugman. The junta of Capá Prieto was as follows: Juan de Mata Terreforte,[66] Vice-President; Pablo Antonio Beauchamp,[67] Treasurer; Baldomero Bauren[68] (sic), Secretary; Francisco Arroyo,[69] brother instructor; Juan Chavarri, agent of relaciones exteriores; and two alternates: Pedro and Eduviges Beauchamp.[70]

Many of the members of these societies were related to each other by blood lines and/or marriage. For example, in the Lares cell, the leaders Rojas, the Pol brothers, Francisco Ramírez, Clemente Millán, and Aurelio Méndez, were all married to the six daughters of José Manuel Serrano, the sexton of the Lares church. Mariana Bracetti was married to Miguel Rojas, a brother of the president of Centro Bravo.[71] in Mayagüez, the Brugmans were related to the Beauchamps and the Arroyos, as two of Brugman's daughters married men from those families. Another daughter, Isabel Brugman, married an overseer in their hacienda, Agustín Lara,[72] also a member of Capá Prieto. Bruno Laracuenta, an hacendado and slave owner, married one of the Arroyo sisters,[73] while Adolfo Betances, brother of Ramón Emeterio, married one of the Terreforte sisters.[74]

Two other societies operating in Puerto Rico in July 1868 were Lanzador del Norte in barrio Palomar, Camuy, and *Porvenir* in the municipality of Pepino (San Sebastián). The junta of the Camuy cell was composed of Manuel María González, President; Bartolomé González Soto,[75] Treasurer; Marcelino Vega,[76] Secretary; Carlos Martínez,[77] brother instructor. We found no information about the posts of vice-president, agents, and alternates in this society. Other well-known members of that society were Pablo Rivera García,[78] the mayor of Camuy, José Cecilio López,[79] a landowner from barrio Ciénega (Camuy), José Antonio Hernández,[80] an hacendado from barrio Piedra Gorda (Camuy), Ramón Estrella,[81] and the Spaniard Bonifacio Aguería.[82]

Unfortunately, there were much fewer details about the nature and composition of the secret society of Pepino, Porvenir. Based on Manuel María González' testimony, we learned that Porvenir was already established by July 1868 and that its president was the *alferez* (second lieutenant) of that town's militia, Manuel Cebollero Aguilar.[83] The society's vice-president was another alferez called Eusebio Ibarra.[84] It is suspected that Juan Nepomuceno Méndez,[85] an itinerant merchant who lived in Pepino, was the society's agent. We have no information about the other members of the junta. We do know, however, about many persons who were members of the organization. Among them were: Cristóbal Castro,[86] the four Font brothers,[87] Cesareo

Martínez,[88] Francisco José Méndez,[89] Clodomiro Euclides Abril,[90] José de los Santos Santiago.[91]

Despite Manuel María González' testimony about the existence of other secret societies in Ponce, Arecibo, Isabela, and San Juan, we found no evidence to show that any of these were in fact in operation prior to the Lares uprising. It is possible that at least in San Juan and in Ponce, where José Celis Aguilera and Carlos Elio Lacroix acted as delegates for the Comité Revolucionario, rebel cells may have been organized, as Eusebio Ibarra testified.[92]

It is also evident that in places such as Arecibo, Yauco, Isabela, Aguada, Añasco, and Vega Baja there were persons who sympathized with the revolutionary cause but who did not take an active part in organizing a rebel society. The rebels' testimonies also indicate that few of them thought they were ready to challenge Spain to war.[93] In the letters Betances wrote to his friends, Justo Barros, Juan Chavarri, and José Francisco Basora, he complained of having been deserted by the creole liberals once he had embraced the cause of revolution.[94] He added that even those who had agreed to participate did little or nothing to propagate the rebel cause. The reasons why the conspirators were having trouble with the revolutionary plan were uncovered by Manuel María González in the Summer of 1868.

According to González, at the end of July he traveled from Camuy to Lares and Mayagüez to ascertain what progress had been made by the rebel organizations there.[95] In Lares, he found Rojas extremely optimistic, claiming he had about 30 or 40 active members in his organization who, in turn, had the support of about 500 to 600 men who were committed to fight when the time came. He assured Gonzalez that they also had some weapons and war materiel stored away, adding that Betances would be bringing more war supplies once the war began. Rojas provided him with a list of persons who were trying to organize rebel cells in other towns.

In Mayagüez, the progress of the revolutionary cause was hampered by doubts. According to Matías Brugman, his cell was doing very well since it had a commitment from the seaman Ramón Pinzón[96] to deliver many sailors to the cause of independence. A similar promise had been made by Juan Chavarri that he would deliver all the artisans of the region. Brugman too assured González that his men were ready and had enough weapons to begin the fight. He mentioned also that they had just ordered more weapons from Betances.

After Brugman, González paid a visit to José (Teclo) Gonce, a member of Capá Prieto. He found Gonce somewhat pessimistic, as he told him that in the beginning there had been great enthusiasm among the members but that now they could not even organize a junta.[97] Distressed by Gonce's assessment, González pressed him for details. Gonce explained that internal divisions had surfaced as not all members agreed on what should be the final solution for Puerto Rico. He added that some members wanted total independence while others wanted annexation with the United States. González then brought up the matter with Juan Chavarri, who agreed with Gonce's evaluation and added that there was also much fear among the members because they were being closely watched by the local authorities.

But despite the doubts expressed by Gonce and Chavarri and those harbored by Betances in the Spring of 1868, the rebel leaders made plans to launch their attack on 29 September 1868. According to a member of Lanzador del Norte, the date and place of attack were decided by the members of Capá Prieto, at Pedro Beauchamp's house, the night of 18 September.[98] He said that it had been the mayagüezanos who chose Camuy as the place to begin the war. The date of the twenty-ninth, according to another witness,[99] was chosen because on that day several hundred slaves from the Mayagüez area would be celebrating outside of the haciendas and could be lured to join their cause. The other factors also considered were that revolutionary movements in Cuba and in Spain were scheduled to begin fighting around the same time. With both places at war, they reasoned it would be hard for the Spanish government to send troops to both Cuba and Puerto Rico if they were also needed in Spain.[100]

In Camuy, where the war cry was to be given, the junta was also plagued by doubts and needed to be reassured. At a meeting held at the house of José Cecilio López, the night of 20 September, many questions were raised by Manuel María Gonzalez and others about the feasibility of the plan. According to several witnesses, Centro Bravo sent its secretary Manuel Ramírez to that meeting to reassure the camuyanos and offer them concrete help. Ramírez confirmed the fact they had many weapons, namely rifles, revolvers, machetes, and gunpowder, with which to hold out until Betances arrived with the new shipment and recruits he was to obtain in Saint Thomas and Santo Domingo. He also promised González that he would receive all the weapons powder, and recruits he needed from Lares and Mayagüez. In what appeared to be a final attempt to push the camuyanos to reach a final decision, Ramírez reminded them that if Camuy refused to give the cry of war, Lares would be happy to do so and take the glory. His words obviously helped since the meeting adjourned with the understanding that Camuy would go first.

NOTES

    1 The islands' special circumstances apparently were tied to their slaves and mixed populations. For a brief, but good discussion on this subject, see Loida Figueroa, *History of Puerto Rico* (New York: Anaya-Las Americas Pub. Co., 1974), p. 261.
    2 For a discussion of this decree, see Lidio Cruz Monclova, *Historia de Puerto Rico (Siglo XIX)* 2nd Edition (Rio Piedras: Editorial Universitaria, 1958) I, pp. 375-376.

3   The result of those elections was as follows: José Julián Acosta, a liberal, and Manuel Valdés Linares, a conservative were elected in the district of San Juan; the delegate for Ponce was Luis Antonio Becerra Delgado, a conservative; for San Germán the man elected was Francisco Mariano Quiñones, a liberal; for Arecibo the delegate was Manuel Zeno Correa, an ultra conservative (conservador puro); for Mayagüez, Segundo Ruiz Belvis, a radical. The result of the elections is discussed in Lidio Cruz Monclova, *Historia*, I, pp. 377-378.

4   In a letter, Betances told Luis Caballer Mendoza of Ponce that the separatists made peace with the liberals and nominated him (Betances) for the district of Mayagüez, but that he had proposed Ruiz Belvis instead since he would provoke less opposition, as he (Betances) had just returned from exile. Excerpts of that letter appear in Cruz Monclova, *Historia*, I, p. 379.

5   The nature of the men chosen for the Puerto Rican commission is described in Loida Figueroa, *History of Puerto Rico*, p. 264.

6   According to Loida Figueroa, Governor Marchesi was very interested in maintaining slavery in Puerto Rico, which is why he chose the conservatives José Ramón Fernández and Juan Bautista Machicote to tip the scales in favor of the *status quo*. Loida Figueroa, *History of Puerto Rico*, pp. 263-264.

7   For details about the political conditions in Spain in the mid-1860s, see Melchor Fernández Almagro, *Historia Política de la España Contemporanea, 1868-1885*, (Madrid: Alianza Editorial, 1969), p. 11.

8   Loida Figueroa, *History of Puerto Rico*, p. 264.

9   For a brief discussion of the report presented by the Cuban delegate, see Loida Figueroa, *History of Puerto Rico*, pp. 269-270.

10   Loida Figueroa, *History of Puerto Rico*, p. 269.

11   The report, drafted by Ruiz Belvis, summarized the history of slavery and presented moral arguments against the system. It also presented arguments to dissuade the fears of the government that emancipation would result in racial upheaval, economic decline and other problems. See the reprinted version: *Proyecto para la abolición de la esclavitud en Puerto Rico* (San Juan: Instituto de Cultura Puertorriqueña, 1959).

12   The tax burden was increased by the government's adoption of the suggestion made by the delegates of levying a direct tax of 6 percent on the net product of agriculture, commerce, and industry. But this tax was simply added to the overburdened taxpayers without removing any of those mentioned by the delegates. Cruz Monclova, *Historia*, I, p. 428.

13   Anecdote related in *Historia de Mayagüez*, p. 305.

14   The case would have promptly been forgotten had Governor Marchesi not interfered, for Colonel Nicolás Rodríguez filed the case after reprimanding the leaders. Marchesi, however, convinced Rodríguez to make an example of the leader, Corporal Benito Montero, by charging him with treason and condemning him to death. The Governor gave Rodríguez his word that he would pardon Montero in time to avoid execution. Rodríguez did as told, but Marchesi did not keep his word and Montero was shot. Colonel Rodríguez committed suicide soon after. The incident is discussed in Cruz Monclova, *Historia*, I, pp. 429-430.

15   The deportation orders were served between 25 June and 5 July 1867. The orders stated that the men in question were to present themselves before the Overseas Minister in Spain. Loida Figueroa, *History of Puerto Rico*, pp. 271-272.

16   The list of men exiled was taken from Cruz Monclova, *Historia*, I, p. 430.

17   Letter from the Governor of Puerto Rico, José Maria Marchesi to the Governor of Cuba, 13 December 1866. A copy of this letter is in AGPR, *Obras Públicas* (Asuntos

Varios), Caja 144, Leg. 181, Entrada No. 21 (Hereafter cited as Marchesi Letter, 13 December 1866).

18   Marchesi Letter, 13 December 1866.

19   Marchesi Letter, 13 December 1866.

20   The Plan presented by Gamir to Marchesi appears reprinted in Cayetano Coll y Toste, *Boletín Histórico de Puerto Rico* Vol. II, pp. 276-283 (Hereafter cited as The Gamir Plan).

21   The Gamir Plan, p. 277.

22   One example of this type of action was the mutiny of the Granada Regiment, stationed in San Juan, in 1835.

23   Marchesi Letter, 13 December 1866.

24   The Gamir Plan, p. 277.

25   The Gamir Plan, Ibid.

26   Letter from Ramón E. Betances to Eladio Ayala, 23 September 1867, reprinted in Luis Bonafoux's *Betances* (San Juan: Instituto de Cultura Puertorriqueña, 1970), pp. 7-72.

27   Betances to Eladio Ayala, 23 September 1867.

28   Betances to Eladio Ayala, 23 September 1867.

29   Letter from Betances to his brother, Adolfo Betances, 24 September 1867, in Bonafoux, Ibid., p. xliv.

30   Betances to Adolfo Betances, 24 September 1867.

31   The charges against Betances and Ruiz Belvis are alluded to in the letter Betances and Ruiz Belvis sent to the *New York Herald*, 3 August 1867, which appears in Pérez Moris, *Historia de la Insurrección de Lares*, 2nd Edition. (Rio Piedras: Editorial Edil, Inc., 1975), p. 59.

32   Cited from Felix Ojeda Reyes, "Diez Meses de Misión Confidencial a Estados Unidos," *Historia y Revolución* (Publicación del Grupo de Investigaciones Históricas del Partido Socialista Puertorriqueño) Año I, No. 1 (Septiembre 1976), p. 9.

33   Letter from José Francisco Basora to Benjamín Vicuña Mackenna, 19 January 1866, reprinted in Ojeda Reyes, "Diez Meses de Misión Confidencial . . . ," pp. 10-11.

34   Letter from Betances to Basora, 14 January 1868, reprinted in Bonafoux, *Betances*, pp. 89-94.

35   Betances to Basora, 14 January 1868, in Bonafoux, *Betances*, p. 90.

36   Betances to Basora, 14 January 1868, in Bonafoux, *Betances*, p. 91.

37   Betances to Basora, 14 January 1868, in Bonafoux, *Betances*, p. 94.

38   Document presented by Aurelio Tío, editor, "La identidad de los restos del patricio Lcdo. Segundo Ruiz Belvis," in *Boletín de la Academia Puertorriqueña de la Historia*, Vol. III, No. 9 (enero 1973), pp. 88-93. For a more recent version, see, Ada Suárez, "Segundo Ruiz Belvis, (Hormigueros, Puerto Rico, 1829-Valparaíso Chile, 1867)" in *Caribe*, Año 11, No. 4 (1982), p. 40.

39   Betances' suspicions were conveyed in letters to relatives of Ruiz Belvis and to his friends. In a letter to Father Meriño, 24 January 1868, Betances requested that he go to Chile to investigate the cause of Ruiz Belvis' death. The letter appears in Bonafoux, *Betances*, pp. 95-97.

40   "Sobre la Muerte de Ruiz Belvis" in Pérez Moris, *Historia de la Insurrección de Lares*, p. 285.

41   "A Los Puertorriqueños" in Bonafoux, *Betances*, pp. 3-5.

42   Ibid., Bonafoux, *Betances*, pp. 4-5.

43   Betances to Pedro Lovera, 18 April 1868, in Bonafoux, *Betances*, p. 77.

44   Betances to José Francisco Basora, 30 April 1868, in Bonafoux, *Betances*, p. 83.

45   Bonafoux, *Betances*, p. 12.

46 A copy of the constitution appears in Bonafoux, *Betances*, pp. 15-20.

47 The structure of the secret societies and the role of each member of the board were described by the rebels during the investigation. For example, see testimony of Manuel María González, Arecibo, 4 November 1868, in AGPR, FGEPR, *La Revolución de Lares 1868*, Caja 181, Pieza 13.

48 A summary of the "Reglamento formado por nosotros los fundadores de la asociación para la litertad e independencia de la Isla de Puerto Rico," (Hereafter cited as Reglamento, Lanzador del Norte) appears in Pérez Moris, *Historia de la Insurrección de Lares*, pp. 77-80.

49 Reglamento, Lanzador del Norte.

50 Reglamento, Lanzador del Norte.

51 The oath is cited in Judge Navascués' *Informe Final*, p. 4 AGPR, FGEPR, *La Revolución de Lares 1868*, Caja 181 (Hereafter cited as Navascués' *Informe Final*); also in Manuel María González' Testimony, 19 October 1868, in Pérez Moris, *Historia de la Insurrección de Lares*, p. 120.

52 Bonafoux, *Betances*, p. 20.

53 The secret gathering is described in Judge Navascués' *Informe Final*, p. 18.

54 A copy of this alphabet was found among the documents that are kept in A.H.N., Madrid, "Documentos . . . Sublevación de Lares," Exp. 20128, Doc. 24.

55 The information about the pseudonyms is found in A.H.N., Madrid, "Documentos . . . Sublevación de Lares." Exp. 20128, Doc. 24, p. 30. Also in Navascués' *Informe Final*, p. 18.

56 Navascués' *Informe Final*, p. 18.

57 Testimony of Francisco Arroyo, Arecibo, 16 December 1868, in *Boletín de Historia Puertorriqueña*, Vol. II, No. 5 (Abril 1950), pp. 159-160.

58 Pérez Moris claims that a member of Capá Prieto named Tomás Turull, was killed by someone in that organization after he betrayed the group by handing over to the Spanish authorities the money collected by the organization and by revealing their plans. For details, see *Historia de la Insurrección de Lares*, p. 85.

59 For Judge Navascués' statements, see his *Informe Final*, p. 20V.

60 Bonafoux, *Betances*, p. 12.

61 José Celis Aguilera was among the eleven men exiled by Governor Marchesi in 1867 and a member of the Comité Revolucionario directed by Betances. The fact that he was never taken prisoner, nor was he in any way incriminated has led some historians to wonder if Aguilera ever did anything for the rebel cause, even if Betances favored him. For a discussion about Aguilera's role, see Bonafoux, *Betances*, p. 9; Loida Figueroa, *History of Puerto Rico*, p. 274; Lidio Cruz Monclova, *Historia*, I, p. 441.

62 Carlos Elio Lacroix was also among those exiled by Governor Marchesi and among those who founded the Comité Revolucionario in the Dominican Republic. Unlike Aguilera, however, Lacroix was captured by the Spanish military troops and subjected to much suffering in the district jail of Aguadilla. For information on Carlos E. Lacroix, see in AGPR, FGEPR, *La Revolución de Lares 1868*, Caja 179, Pieza 39; also in Caja 181, Piezas 47, 48.

63 The mission assigned to Chavarri by the Comité included the powers of a "special" agent, to organize societies, ratify nominations for presidencies of the societies, and head the meetings of those societies lacking recognized leadership. His role in the Comité Revolucionario was to act as courier and liaison between that organization and the societies on the island. He participated in the Lares uprising and escaped to the Dominican Republic despite the strict vigilance of the Spanish coast guard. For Chavarri's assignment, see Bonafoux, *Betances*, p. 11; for his role in the plot and uprising, see in AGPR, FGEPR, *La Revolución de Lares 1868*, Caja 181, Pieza 48.

64   The names and the positions occupied by these rebels in the secret society of Lares were compiled from various sources. The most useful of them being the "Estado Demostrativo de los procesados . . . ," AGPR, FGEPR, *La Revolución de Lares 1868*, Caja 181, Piezas 47, 48.

65   AGPR, FGEPR, *La Revolución de Lares 1868*, Caja 181, Piezas 47, 48.

66   Juan de Mata Terreforte was a photographer and owned a small business in barrio Furnias (Mayagüez). In 1895 he was among a group of Puerto Rican patriots in New York City who formed the *Sección Puerto Rico del Partido Revolucionario Cubano*.

67   Pablo Antonio Beauchamp was the owner of the hacienda *Guavas* in Furnias (Mayagüez). He owned slaves, four of whom he sent to fight in the Lares uprising as a condition for granting them their liberty. According to the income-tax form he submitted for 1866-67, Beauchamp owned 875 cuerdas of land, nine slaves, and other property not detailed, assessed at 30,000 pesos. His hacienda produced mostly coffee and food crops. For the records of hacienda Guavas, see in AMM, Docs. Mun., 1866, Vol. 2.

68   Betances spelled Baldomero's last name as Bauring. He was a Dominican acting as a secret agent in Puerto Rico, who was shot by the Spanish troops. He worked for Matías Brugman as an overseer in his hacienda, and operated under the pseudonym *Guayubín*. The spelling of Bauring is found in the "Acta" the Comité Revolucionario drafted on 24 February 1868, in Bonafoux, *Betances*, p. 13.

69   Francisco Arroyo was married to Matías Brugman's youngest daughter Petra. He was also an hacendado in Mayagüez. See Arturo Brugman's interview in *La Correspondencia*, 28 February 1941, p. 24.

70   Pedro and Eduviges were brother and sister, members of the wealthy Beauchamp family. Pedro was one of the society's agents, or aides to the president and Eduviges was honored with the title of "distinguished member." She was at the time of the uprising confused with Mariana Bracetti and credited with making the revolutionary flag, and called *Brazo de Oro* (Golden Arm), a name also given to the female patriot of Lares by the rebels of *Centro Bravo*. For the place the Beauchamps occupied in Mayagüez, see AMM, Docs. Mun., 1866, Vol. 2. For their role in the rebel society, see Navascués' *Informe Final*, p. 2.

71   Information compiled from the rebels testimonies in AGPR, FGEPR, *La Revolución de Lares 1868*, Caja 176-181, Several Piezas.

72   Details about the Brugman's marriages, in Arturo Brugman's interview in *La Correspondencia*, 28 Febrero 1941, p. 24.

73   Bruno Laracuenta owned a 400 cuerdas estancia, named "La Florida" in barrio Furnias (Mayagüez), assessed at 16,000 pesos. He also owned four slaves, horses, and four cows. For details about Laracuenta's property holdings, see in AMM, Docs. Mun., 1866, Vols. 1, 2. For his participation in the uprising see in AGPR, FGEPR, *La Revolución de Lares 1868*, Caja 181, Piezas 47, 48.

74   Adolfo Betances' Testimony, Aguadilla, 26 October 1868, in AGPR, FGEPR, *La Revolución de Lares 1868*, Caja 177, Pieza 11.

75   González Soto, according to his own testimony (1 October 1868), was born in Pepino (San Sebastián) but lived in Camuy, where he joined the rebel organization Lanzador del Norte. He defined himself as a "labrador propietario" (one who owned so little land that he was forced to augment his income by working part of the year for others). His testimony appears in AGPR, FGEPR, *La Revolución de Lares 1868*, Caja 177, Pieza 11. The information about the slave he bought is in AGPR, *Prot. Not., Lares 1867*, Caja 1424, f. 54.

76   Marcelino Vega, like Manuel María González, was born in Venezuela and earned a living as a small retail merchant, in barrio Camuy Arriba (Camuy). Like so many other rebels, Vega was bankrupt by 1868. The details about Vega's origin and role

in the secret society are from AGPR, FGEPR, *La Revolución de Lares 1868*, Caja 181, Piezas 47, 48. The details about his economic status are from AGPR, *Prot. Not.*, Series: Arecibo, Municipality: *Camuy 1869*, Caja 1702, ff. 54, 75, 187-188.

77 Carlos Martínez was born in Aguadilla and lived in Camuy at the time of the Lares uprising. He earned his living by practicing medicine without a license. He was charged by the authorities for starting the armed struggle following the arrest of Manuel María González. See in AGPR, FGEPR, *La Revolución de Lares 1868*, Caja 181, Piezas 47-48.

78 Pablo Rivera García was born in Naguabo (Puerto Rico) and lived in Camuy, where he served as mayor of the municipal government. He was charged with belonging to the secret society Lanzador del Norte, AGPR, FGEPR, *La Revolución de Lares 1868*, Caja 181, Piezas 47, 48. According to the notarial records of Lares, Rivera García owned several hundred cuerdas of land in Lares, Adjuntas, and Utuado. In March 1867 he sold an estancia of 300 cuerdas, with a house, a place of storage, a sugar mill (trapiche), and all the equipment for making sugar, with some cuerdas planted in coffee, plantains, and sugar cane, for the total sum of 16,000 pesos (32,000 escudos), accepting in lieu of a cash downpayment five slaves worth 2,846 pesos in AGPR, *Prot. Not., Lares 1867*, Caja 1424, f. 82.

79 José Cecilio López was born in Aguadilla (Puerto Rico) and resided in Camuy. According to Manuel María González' testimony (Arecibo, 20 October 1868), López refused to join the rebel cell, but volunteered to aid the families of members who met with misfortune. López was one of the 70 plus rebels who died in jail. Details about Lopez' promise and fate, in AGPR, FGEPR, *La Revolución de Lares 1868*, Caja 181, Piezas 47, 48. A copy of Manuel María González' testimony appears in Pérez Moris, *Historia de la Insurrección de Lares*, pp. 115-120, whereas reference to that testimony appears in the testimony of the rebel Andrés Corcino González, Aguadilla, 16 January, in AGPR, FGEPR, *La Revolución de Lares 1868*, Caja 179, Pieza 40.

80 Hernández was born and lived in Camuy, where he owned an estancia. He was a member of the secret society Lanzador del Norte, for which he kept, buried in his farm, 1,000 cartridges. Hernández was among the first to be captured by the Spanish troops after the armed attack ended. He died in jail on 6 November 1868, in AGPR, FGEPR, *La Revolución de Lares 1868*, Caja 173, Pieza 13 and Caja 181, Piezas 47, 48.

81 Estrella was a pulpero (small retail merchant) in Camuy. He was born in Aguadilla (Puerto Rico) and belonged to Lanzador del Norte. He was apparently the agent for that society, for the Spaniards charged him with "acquiring and disseminating news" among the rebels, a function generally performed by the "agente de relaciones exteriores." AGPR, FGEPR, *La Revolución de Lares 1868*, Caja 181, Piezas 47, 48.

82 Aguería was born in Asturias, Spain and lived in Hatillo, Puerto Rico. Aguería was a member of Lanzador del Norte and was sent to the district jail of Arecibo. AGPR, FGEPR, *La Revolución de Lares 1868*, Caja 181, Piezas 47, 48.

83 Cebollero was born in Aguada (Puerto Rico) and lived in Pepino where he earned his living as a shopkeeper. Cebollero cooperated with the authorities after he was arrested and avoided being court martialed and possibly sentenced to death as were several other leaders of the conspiracy. See Cebollero's testimony in *Boletín de Historia Puertorriqueña*, Vol. II, No. 7 (Junio 1950), pp. 195-196. For the details about his place of birth and involvement in the conspiracy and revolt, see in AGPR, FGEPR, *La Revolución de Lares 1868*, Caja 181, Piezas 47, 48.

84 Ironically, Ibarra's pseudonym was *Esperanza* (Hope), yet he was the best informer the courts had. He gave the authorities every name and recounted every conversation he had heard concerning the conspiracy and revolt. See Ibarra's many testimonies in AGPR, FGEPR, *La Revolución de Lares 1868*, Caja 177, Pieza 11, Caja 178, Pieza 12,

Caja 179, Pieza 13; also see his testimony in *Boletín de Historia Puertorrinqueña*, Ibid., p. 194-195. For his participation in the society, see in AGPR, FGEPR, Caja 181, Piezas 47, 48.

85 Méndez was charged with inciting a group of men to fight against the Spanish troops, on 24 September 1868. He was known among the rebels by the pseudonym *Bronce*. See AGPR, FGEPR, *La Revolución de Lares 1868*, Caja 181, Piezas 47, 48. According to the notarial records of San Sebastián, Méndez lost a small store and four cuerdas of land he owned in barrio Piedras Blancas (San Sebastián) to don Juan Medina, his creditor. In AGPR, *Prot. Not., San Sebastián 1870*, f. 224. His part in the conspiracy, in AGPR, FGEPR, *La Revolución de Lares 1868*, Caja 181, Piezas 47.

86 Don Cristobal Castro was born in the Canary Islands, Spain and lived in Pepino. Don Cristobal sold in 1870 an estancia of 109 cuerdas of land he purchased from Manuel Reyes in 1865. That sale, like so many made by the rebels, was made to pay back payments. In AGPR, *Prot. Not., San Sebastián 1870*, Caja 1473, f. 107.

87 According to the notarial records of San Sebastián, Manuel, Miguel, Ramón and Rodrigo Font worked on the family lands. Only Miguel had any record of buying and selling property between 1866 and 1870. In January 1866, the notary of San Sebastián recorded that Miguel Font ceded to Amell, Juliá y Co. of Aguadilla eight cuerdas of land he had just bought from José Antonio Medina to pay 464 escudos he owed that firm. In AGPR, Prot. Not., *San Sebastián 1866*, Caja 1470, f. 9.

88 Martínez was a member of Porvenir, charged with firing at the Lares merchant, don Antonio Ferrer, and taking his horse, and ordering several owners of slaves to free them. Martínez was born and lived in Pepino. He earned his living as a cigarmaker. He was also a musician. For these details, see in AGPR, FGEPR. *La Revolución de Lares 1868*, Caja 181, Piezas 47, 48.

89 Méndez was born in Moca (Puerto Rico) and resided in Pepino. He belonged to Porvenir and at the time of the uprising was responsible for recruiting between 200-300 men. In AGPR, FGEPR, *La Revolución de Lares 1868*, Caja 181, Piezas 47, 48.

90 Clodomiro E. Abril was born in San Juan (Puerto Rico) and lived in Pepino, where he worked as a scribe for the municipal government. He was a member of the secret society Porvenir and was that society's choice for the post of Overseas Minister in the republican government. He was court martialed and sentenced to death for his participation in the conspiracy and revolt. In AGPR, FGEPR, *La Revolución de Lares 1868*, Caja 181, Piezas 47, 48; court martial and death sentence, in Ibid., *Audiencia Territorial, Tribunal Pleno*, Caja 7.

91 Santiago was born in Pepino, but lived in nearby Adjutas. In the notarial records of San Sebastián it was recorded in October 1867 that Santiago was pushed to sell an estancia of 75 cuerdas he owned in barrio Guayo (Utuado) to pay his creditor, Sociedad Joaquín Ferrer y Co. of Lares, 4,000 escudos. In AGPR, *Prot. Not., San Sebastián 1867*, Caja 1427, f. 315.

92 Testimony of Eusebio Ibarra, Arecibo, 31 October 1868, in AGPR, FGEPR, Caja 178, Pieza 12.

93 See Manuel María González' testimonies given in Arecibo, 20 October 1868, in Pérez Moris, op. cit., p. 119; 4 November 1868 in AGPR, FGEPR, *La Revolución de Lares 1868*, Caja 178, Pieza 13.

94 Bonafoux, *Betances*, pp. 77-81.

95 González' Testimony, 20 October 1868, in Pérez Moris, *Historia de la Insurrección*, pp. 115-120.

96 Details about Pinzón also appear in the interrogations made by Judge Navascués, in Arecibo, 22, 27 October 1868 which are found in AGPR, FGEPR, *La Revolución de Lares 1868*, Caja 178, Pieza 13. Pinzón denied all charges made against him by

Manuel María González. Pinzón was born in Santo Domingo and lived in Mayagüez. He was a sailor of about 40 years of age.

97 See González' Testimony, in Pérez Moris, *Historia de la Insurrección*, p. 118.

98 Testimony of Ramón Estrella, Arecibo, 3 November 1868, in AGPR, FGEPR, *La Revolución de Lares 1868*, Caja 178, Pieza 13.

99 Testimony of Bartolomé González Soto, 4 November 1868, in AGPR, FGEPR, *La Revolución de Lares 1868*, Caja 178, pieza 13.

100 Testimony of José Antonio Hernández, Arecibo, 4 November 1868, in AGPR, FGEPR, *La Revolución de Lares 1868*, Caja 178, Pieza 13.

IV
The Republic Is Proclaimed

Unknown to the rebels of Camuy, on the night of 20 September, while they plotted to overthrow the Spanish government, the military commander of Arecibo, Colonel Manuel de Iturriaga, planned to capture their leader Manuel María González, and put an end to the impending revolt.[1] The indiscretion of a member of Lanzador del Norte led to the discovery of the plot.

On the morning of 20 September, a young creole named Carlos Antonio López, stationed in the militia headquarters in Quebradillas, visited his compatriot, Captain Juan Castañón,[2] to tell him that his uncle, Hilario Martínez, had informed him that "a conspiracy was being planned in the home of Manuel María Gonzalez [President of Lanzador del Norte], for the purpose of starting a revolution to free the island from Spain."[3] Intrigued by López's story, Castañón pressed for details. He had to be sure who was involved before he could move to arrest them.

Castañón thanked López and asked him not to tell anyone about their meeting. He promised that he would soon take care of the matter.[4]

To avoid a jurisdictional conflict between the military and the civilian authorities in the district, Castañón decided to share the news of the conspiracy with the mayor of Quebradillas, Carlos González. He needed his cooperation in capturing the conspirators.[5]

Carlos González, in turn, notified Castañón that he would have to alert the mayor of Camuy, since the suspects were under his jurisdiction. Was González in fact observing the rules of jurisdiction? Or was he, as Castañón suspected, buying time to warn the rebels of Camuy? The latter seems more probable for González was very eager to get to Camuy.[6] He arrived at the *Casa del Rey* around twelve noon, Sunday, 20 September. Finding the mayor, Pablo Rivera, accompanied by the Captain of the Camuy Militia, Francisco Alcazar, González asked for a room where they could speak privately.[7] What they actually said Alcazar did not hear, but he remembered that they talked for about 15 minutes behind closed doors.

As soon as González left, Alcazar questioned Rivera about the purpose of the sudden and mysterious visit. Rivera, apparently unnerved, told Alcazar the whole story, adding that González had come to seek advice on how he and Castañón should proceed.[8] Pressed for details, Rivera said that he advised them to inform Colonel Manual de Iturriaga, in Arecibo. Alcazar added that shortly after this incident he saw Pablo Rivera write a long letter, which he later sent to Lares.[9]

Meanwhile, in Quebradillas, Juan Castañón awaited González' decision. At four in the afternoon he went to see González for the second time that day. González, Castañón reported, appeared to be stalling and asked him for a written report so that he could proceed with the plans to arrest the rebels of Camuy. He made no mention of Pablo Rivera's suggestion to inform Colonel Iturriaga.

Suspicious of González, Castañón decided not to wait any longer. Instead, he saddled his horse and took off for Arecibo to warn his superior about the impending revolt.[10] He arrived at the military headquarters of Arecibo by nightfall. Soon after, Iturriaga gave orders to organize a small expedition to search the home of Manuel María Gonzales that very night. Iturriaga then took his men through the town of Camuy, where he not only obtained a search warrant from Mayor Pablo Rivera, but demanded that he join the expedition. It was nearly three in the morning when they reached Manuel María González' house in barrio Palomar, Camuy.[11]

Everyone was sound asleep, including the guard whose duty it was to alert the president of the rebel cell in cases such as this. Perhaps they were more tired than usual, for that night they had been at José Cecilio López' house, in barrio Ciénega, planning the date when the armed struggle was to begin.[12]

Colonel Iturriaga awakened the González family and subjected the President of Lanzador del Norte to a four-hour interrogation about the conspiracy, without any results.[13] In the meantime, Mayor Pablo Rivera and other members of Iturriaga's expedition were ordered to search the house. They found no incriminating evidence and Iturriaga decided to look for himself. He found what he needed. In an old ledger, originally inspected by Mayor Rivera, Iturriaga found several coded documents related to the conspiracy.[14] One of them was a list of the members of the Lanzador del Norte. Another contained the society's rules and regulations, called the *Reglamento formado por nosotros los fundadores de la asociación para la libertad e independencia de la isla de Puerto Rico*. There were also several notes González had written to himself about the need of obtaining arms.[15]

With that evidence, Iturriaga proceeded to arrest Manuel María González and to take him to the district jail in Arecibo the morning of September 21st.[16] News of González' arrest spread quickly and by the afternoon of the 21st several members of Lanzador del Norte gathered at the home of Carlos Martínez. Martínez, the brother instructor of the rebel cell, was in this case the man with the power to decide what was to be done. He decided to rescue González from his jailers.[17]

According to José Antonio Hernández, not present, but informed of the results of the meeting, about one in the afternoon of the 21st a group of 40 or 50 armed men, from Lanzador del Norte, visited his farm demanding that he follow them to Camuy. The purpose was to catch up with Iturriaga's expedition, rescue the prisoner, kill the guards, take all the weapons and munitions kept in the militia garrison in Camuy, and give the cry for independence.[18]

Hernández, by his own admission argued with Carlos Martínez about the wisdom of such a decision and refused to follow him. Martínez then threatened to kill him and Hernández, feigning a change of heart, promised to do as told as soon as he could get his men together. But after Martínez left, Hernández, according to his workers, went into hiding and advised them to do the same.[19]

By then Carlos Martínez had apparently changed his mind about rescuing González. Instead he took his men through barrio Puertos (Camuy) and headed for Lares. News of Martínez' moves were reported to Colonel Iturriaga that afternoon by members of the Spanish colony in barrio Palomar (Camuy). Claiming that a rebellion had broken out in barrio Puertos, the Spaniards requested military troops to protect their lives and estates. Iturriaga sent 50 militiamen from Camuy and 25 Spanish soldiers, under the command of Captain José Pujols. The troops searched Puertos the evening of the 21st and, finding nothing out of the ordinary, returned to their posts.[20] Martínez had already gone to Lares to discuss the arrest of González with the President of Centro Bravo, Manuel Rojas.

The news brought by Carlos Martínez forced Rojas to take action at once. First, he had to notify the President of Capá Prieto, Matías Brugman and the rebel members in Mayagüez. Second, Carlos Martínez would have to return to Camuy to organize his troops and secure the gunpowder and cartridges buried in José Antonio Hernández' farm. Third, members of other secret cells had to be notified that the date for the attack had been moved forward. Fourth, the men at Centro Bravo would have to begin preparations for an immediate war.[21]

Meanwhile, in Arecibo the guards interrogated Manuel María González and Iturriaga tried to decipher the coded documents he seized from González.

In Mayagüez, Brugman agreed with Rojas' conclusion that it was best to act quickly. He called a meeting at his house for the following evening (September 22nd). It would take the whole day to round up the leaders in the nearby barrios. The meeting ended early since Brugman presented a ready-made plan the members quickly agreed on. It required that they take up arms the next day, declare Puerto Rico independent, rescue Manuel María González, and then join forces with the men of Camuy, Lares and Pepino.[22] The reasons for this strategy were well-known to those present; they needed the weapons and munitions of the militias in those municipalities before they could proceed to Arecibo, which was a military stronghold.[23]

The meeting adjourned with the understanding that those present would notify other members and return the next morning with their slaves, their workers, friend and relatives willing to join the rebels' cause. Eugenio Bernard, a member of Capá Prieto, remembered being told of the plans to invade Lares the night of the 22nd by Eugenio and Bruno Chabrier.[24]

Back in Lares and Pepino the leaders of the rebel cells were also spreading the word that the attack would begin the following day. In Pepino, Cebollero and Ibarra, were so enthusiastic that their men took time out to celebrate. The neighbors of the nearby barrios told the authorities that on the night of the 22nd they had heard Ibarra's name hailed several times.[25]

The Day the Republic was Declared

The morning of September 23rd Lares seemed more active than usual, according to the Spanish merchant Frutos Caloca. He recalled seeing early that morning his neighbors Andrés Pol and Francisco Santana escorting their families out of town. Knowing that such measures were taken in Lares only during times of plagues, war, or other emergencies, he decided to remain alert. His suspicions were further aroused when he later saw Manuel Rojas in town buying enormous amounts of food, drinks, and blankets, under the flimsy excuse that he was giving a big party that night.[26]

At Rojas' hacienda everyone was busy preparing for the night's event. Some were sharpening their machetes and knives, while others oiled the pistols and revolvers and made cartridges from the gun powder buried in Rojas' farm. Rojas and the leaders of Porvenir worked out the last minute details of their military plan, reviewed their forces, and generally made sure things would go according to plan.[27]

His visit to Lares involved more than just shopping for supplies, since upon returning to the hacienda, he ordered several guards to patrol the exits leading to Lares, Arecibo, Aguadilla and other urban centers which had military troops. The guards were instructed to apprehend any Spaniard trying to break through the lines.

In the meantime, in Mayagüez, Brugman and Bruno Chabrier were busy in their own haciendas gathering weapons and men to send to Lares that afternoon. According to the hacendado Eugenio Bernard, one of the few Mayagüez rebels who came on horseback, with saber, revolver, and rifle, men had been gathering at Chabrier's house since daybreak.[28] Bernard and his overseer, Pedro Segundo García, arrived about nine-thirty in the morning. Also present were Brugman's stepson, José Antonio Muse, who had brought along some of his slaves, the brothers Pedro and Pablo Beauchamp, also with a number of their slaves, the merchants Juan Bautista Ramírez and Juan Vicentí. About 30 or 40 others, Bernard said, had horses, rifles, revolvers and sabers, as he did.

At Bruno Chabrier's, orders were given by Juan de Mata Terreforte, the emerging military leader, to round up the jornaleros in the nearby haciendas and take them to Lares. As they came in, they were given machetes and told the reasons why they were being recruited.[29] The men on horseback, the slave Cándido remembered, simply ordered the jornaleros and slaves to leave their work and follow them to Lares.[30] Many of those recruited later testified that they were forced to join the leaders of Capá Prieto or they would have been shot.

According to Polinario (one of José Antonio Muse's slaves ordered to fight), the rebels of Maygüez were divided into two groups: those on horseback, who were generally small hacendados, farmers, and retail merchants from the rural areas; those on foot, who were mostly jornaleros and slaves. The mounted men, he remembered, were the best equipped, for they carried at least a rifle, a pistol or revolver, and a saber. Those on foot carried only the machetes they were given by the leaders.[31]

Among those giving orders, the jornaleros remembered the hacendado, Francisco (Paco) Arroyo. At least 20 jornaleros claimed to have been ordered to join the rebel ranks by Paco Arroyo. They claimed that he and other leaders threatened them with their revolvers.[32] This story of coercion was later used by the Spanish authorities to convince the inhabitants of Puerto Rico that the revolutionary cause did not have grass-roots support.[33]

It should be added, however, that while some jornaleros and slaves were indeed coerced, others joined voluntarily as soon as they were asked to do so by their employers.[34] It seems that coercion was used by the leaders with those workers and slaves belonging to haciendas whose owners either opposed or could not be trusted to join the revolutionary plot. The possibility also exists that, once captured, the jornaleros, fearing for their lives and their jobs, made up the stories about coercion. It should be remembered that even if they survived the ordeal of Spanish justice they still had to face their employers, upon whose mercy they depended for work and a plot of land.

On the afternoon of 23 September Juan de Mata Terreforte led about 100 men out of Mayagüez.[35] The 18-mile ride to join Rojas' rebels in Lares started out well. Most of the men were singing: "long live liberty."[36] The slave Santana recalled that everyone seemed in a good mood despite the fact that they were so poorly armed to face the Spanish troops. They had also eaten very little that day. No one had remembered to feed the rebel troops. They had been given a couple of shots of rum at the hacienda of Bruno Chabrier. Their only provisions, according to Santana, were some cheese and crackers someone had packed onto two mules.[37]

Terreforte's rebel army stopped several times along the way, to pick up jornaleros working in nearby fields. They were told: "come with us, come to defend our freedom, if you owe anything it will be forgotten because your libreta will be taken away from you." To those who appeared unconvinced, the leaders reminded them how hard they worked and how they could not get out of debt. They added that this condition was caused by the existing government and that it would change if they joined their revolutionary cause.[38]

Official sources say that they also stopped at the house of Manuel Gómez, where they were given more rum, and at the store of the Spaniard Coll, where they ate, drank, sacked the store, and took prisoner its only clerk.[39]

They finally reached Rojas' hacienda around supper time. They were met by Rojas' men, with food and drink for all. It was time for the men and horses to rest until Pedro Pablo González arrived with his group from Adjuntas. Terreforte, Rojas and the other military leaders reviewed their plans.[40]

In Adjuntas, Pedro Pablo González gathered about 20 jornaleros and took off for Lares the night of September 23rd. They reached Rojas' hacienda around ten that evening, after a relatively uneventful march.[41] Everyone in that group apparently came voluntarily since there is no mention of coercive recruitment in this case.[42]

Notified of Gonzalez' arrival, Rojas emerged from his house carrying a red flag. Next to him appeared Clemente Millán with a white flag.[43] Rojas was dressed for the occasion in a makeshift uniform. He wore a red woolen shirt and dark jacket, cashmere pants, riding boots, a revolver, a saber, and a Panama hat bedecked with a cockade of black, white, yellow and red ribbons.[44] Standing in the doorway Rojas spoke to the troops outside about the injustices committed by the government in power and of the necessity to bring it down. He reminded them of the exorbitant taxes, the corruption of the officials, and of their duty to end this tyrannical rule. He promised that, under the revolutionary government, no one would have to pay taxes. The poor jornaleros would have their debts cancelled, and to prove this, he urged them to destroy their libretas, the documents attesting to their bondage.[45]

The speech ended with everyone singing *Death to Spain, Long Live Liberty, Long Live Free Puerto Rico*. At that point, Manuel Cebollero, president of Porvenir, took the white flag from Millán and upon it inscribed, with his cigar, the words being chanted: *Liberty or Death. Long Live Free Puerto Rico. Year 1868*. The jornaleros, moved by Cebollero's gesture, put their libretas to the torch. Rojas announced himself commanding general of the troops and gave orders to follow him to seize the town government of Lares.[46]

About 600 rebels,[47] according to José Antonio Muse, were organized into two columns and led by Manuel Rojas and Juan de Mata Terreforte into Lares. Along the three miles were many Spanish stores, which they attacked. They made prisoners of the Spanish merchants and their clerks, and seized their horses, weapons and munitions. One of the first Spanish merchants to suffer the rebels' wrath was Felipe Arana.[48] His store was sacked by the rebel infantry which took the machetes and knives and drank the wine and beer. The rebel leaders also took the horse and mounting gear, belonging to Arana, and enlisted those who showed up. One who refused to follow them and was shot was the free black man Agustín Venero.[49]

Next, Rojas, Joaquín Parrilla, and Gabino Plumey began to arrest several other Spanish merchants. Among the first to be taken was Pedro Gandarillas. He recalled having been taken from his house, half dressed and barefoot, with hands tied behind his back, to the town's jail, where he was put on the stocks. He stated also that he could have avoided his fate had he a-greed to declare himself in favor of the island's independence as the rebels demanded.[50]

Gandarillas was one of about 20 Spaniards from Lares who suffered such a treatment at the hands of the rebels. It was suspected that Rojas' men were especially hard on Gandarillas because they believed he spied for the government. Others also jailed that night by the rebels were Pablo Media-villa, the mayor of Lares, his assistant, Lorenzo Camuñas, the merchants Bartolomé Bernal, and Francisco Ferret.[51] One merchant the rebels wanted, who managed to escape, was Frutos Caloca. Besides suspecting Caloca of spying for the military authorities in Aguadilla, many of the rebels were indebted to Caloca. But Caloca was nowhere to be found. He went into hiding when he heard the rebels approaching his house. He told Judge Navascués during the investigations that he escaped by jumping out of his bedroom window. Dressed only in his underwear and barefoot, Caloca took a gun and hid in the nearby coffee bushes all night.[52]

Was it fear that forced Caloca and others to hide the night of September 23rd? Or was it acquiescence? Rojas' troops did not enter the town of Lares until midnight, but preparations for the occupation of the town had been going on for at least two days. Yet everyone in the town seemed to be asleep when they stormed the town. Only the mayor and his assistant bothered to leave their beds to inquire what the commotion was all about. It is hard to believe, as Pérez Moris insists, that Rojas' guards sealed the roads so effec-tively that no one could get out.[53] Why didn't any of the merchants fire in their own defense? They all had weapons in their homes and stores. They also had men under their command who could have countered the attack.[54] Is it possible that the inhabitants of Lares approved of the rebels' plans? Per-haps they, too, felt that a change in government was necessary.

Between midnight and three in the morning Rojas' men occupied many of the major Spanish stores in town. According to the druggist, Fidel Navas, who slept in Frutos Caloca's store, a group of men forced their way into that establishment shortly after midnight, shouting "Long Live Free Puerto Rico, Death to the Spaniards, Long Live the Republic."[55] His companions, the clerk Cristabal Bose, and the guard, Ignacio Balbino Ostolaza disappeared when they heard the noise, leaving him alone to face the mob. Navas also recalled that a group led by Leopoldo Plumey surrounded him and threatened his life. Had it not been for the shoemaker, José Arce (alias Chana), who recognized him as the town's druggist, he claimed he would have been killed. As it turned out, Navas was escorted by José Arce to the militia headquarters to treat a wounded rebel named Carlos Feliciano.[56]

On the way to the militia headquarters, Navas reported seeing hundreds of "colored" men in the stores, eating, drinking, and ordering cloth and other goods, for which they did not pay. In Casa Marquez y Co., where he stopped to buy some gauze to bandage the wounded, two black men threatened him with their machetes, but were persuaded not to hurt him by his escort, José Arce. After he had dressed Feliciano's wound, Navas was jailed for the night with the rest of the Spaniards taken prisoners that evening.

Meanwhile, another group of rebels led by Rojas threatened the merchant Antonio Ferrer, ordering him to give himself up in the name of the Republic, and to hand over his four revolvers and horse.[57] Ferrer was immediately taken to jail by Cesareo Martínez.

It was estimated that before the night was over the rebels had cost the merchants about 20,000 pesos in damages and confiscated property.[58]

The estimates of the damages were made by the merchants themselves and are thus subject to question. But, it is undeniable that the rebels did sack and loot the stores of many Spaniards in Lares. Both Francisco Ramírez, later president of the Republic, and Federico Valencia who became Minister of the Treasury, testified to having witnessed such events.

It was nearly two in the morning when Rojas, Terreforte, Ramírez, Millán and several others took possession of City Hall.[59]

With the Spanish merchants and government officials behind bars the rebels proceeded to rid the town hall of the symbols of the Spanish rule. They substituted them with those of the independent Republic of Puerto Rico. For example, the picture of Queen Isabel was replaced by the red and white flags carried by Rojas and Millán into battle. Once the obvious signs of Spanish sovereignty were removed the leaders Rojas, Terreforte, Pol, Millán and Ramírez gathered to draft some laws and choose the members of a provisional government for the Republic.[60]

The Republican Government is Installed

According to the chosen President, Francisco Ramírez, the new government came into existence by appointment.[61] Manuel Rojas and Juan de Mata Terreforte chose the various heads of state the morning of 24 September. Clemente Millán was named Minister (Secretary) of Justice; Federico Valencia became Minister of the Treasury; Aurelio Méndez, Minister of Foreign Relations; and Bernabé Pol was appointed Secretary of State. The new officials were then instructed by Rojas and Terreforte to accept their posts, to recruit more men for the revolution, and to obtain forced loans from the merchants, to subsidize the war.[62]

Next, Rojas and Terreforte named the military commanders who were to lead the troops into Pepino later that morning. The eight division generals named were: Mariano Rocafort, Juaquín Parrilla, Juan Francisco Dorval Beauchamp, Andrés Pol, Gabino Plumey, Matías Brugman, and the brothers Francisco and Rafael Arroyo. Several others were appointed to various posts in the artillery, infantry and cavalry.

With ministers, generals, and other dignitaries assigned to their jobs, the revolutionary government became official as the leaders declared the end of Spanish rule in Puerto Rico. They declared Puerto Rico an independent, sovereign state and threatened to imprison anyone who opposed the new government. They warned that the Spaniards living in Puerto Rico "had three days to declare themselves in favor of the Republic, to leave for Spain, or to accept the punishment reserved for traitors." This decree, along with several others, was signed by the Secretary of State Bernabé Pol and posted on the walls of the buildings in Lares. The first official statement of the revolutionary government concerning the status of the creoles, foreigners and slaves in the republic stated:

We, the members of the Government, making use of our powers, declare: (1) that every son of this country is required to take up arms, to help secure the freedom and independence of Puerto Rico; (2) that any person, of any other nation, that voluntarily takes up arms in favor of our cause, will be accepted as a patriot; (3) that any slave that takes up arms in our favor, will be free by that very act; (4) that those slaves found to be incapacitated will also be freed. Lares, September 23, 1868. (Signed) Bernabé Pol, Secretary of the Ministerio de Gobierno.[63]

The warning they issued to the Spaniards was perhaps a bit premature, if we consider the fact that they had only captured the small town of Lares. But it was the kind of warning that, given the long history of creole subordination, was understandable and necessary.

On the other hand, the decree aimed at the other inhabitants was a calculated attempt to attract other members of the society. By addressing the issue of slavery the revolutionary government appealed to the colored population as well as to the enlightened sector of the society which was against the slave system. To abolish slavery was in the patriots' best interest, as it would lure to their cause thousands of freedmen, as well as those favoring abolition. But the decree was limited in scope, stating that freedom would be granted to those who fought for it and to those physically unfit to fight. What about the rest of the slaves? Would they continue in bondage after the island became free? Is it possible that the rebel leaders, many of whom owned slaves, preferred a slow, piecemeal abolition? Or had the Spanish propaganda about the savagery of the black race had its impact on the patriots, making them worry unnecessarily about their hegemony once the Spaniards were no longer in control. The real impact of this decree will never be known, for the armed struggle did not last long enough for the colored population to consider the merits of joining or opposing the rebels.

Within hours of the first decree, President Francisco Ramírez issued another. Its purpose was to end the semi-slave system of the libretas that had been oppressing the free laborers since 1849. This document, addressed to the hacendado Silvestre González, said:

> Fatherland, Justice, Freedom. Long Live Free Puerto Rico! Soon after you receive this (you) shall request all residents of that barrio who carry libretas to come to this town (Lares) with them so that they can be removed (from them) forever; so that they can be in absolute freedom to choose, free of the yoke that oppresses them. . . .[64]

It is important to note that while both groups of jornaleros and slaves were addressed within hours of the creation of the new government, the emancipation offered to the jornaleros was not restricted by *a priori* conditions. Nowhere in the second decree does it state that fighting in favor of the cause of independence was a necessary condition for the cancellation of the libretas.

Having dealt with the problems of the laboring class, the president concentrated on the questions of increasing the rebel forces, obtaining horses for their transport, and securing food for the troops. Thus, he sent the following written order to the hacendado Juan López of barrio Bartolo:

> Having been elected president of this government by the chiefs of the revolution that has taken command of this town, I advise you to immediately send me one hundred men from that barrio, twelve cows or more, and six horses. (Let me) warn you that if you do not do as told, (you) will be punished severely. Lares September 24, 1868. (Signed) Francisco Ramirez.[65]

In the meantime, the troops led by Manuel Rojas and Juan de Mata Terreforte made their way to the town of Pepino. To insure their success, and perhaps as a sign of gratitude for their victory thus far, the president, Francisco Ramírez, ordered his secretary, Bernabé Pol, to request the priest of Lares, José Gumersindo Vega, to sing a *Te Deum*.[66] Between seven and eight in the morning of 24 September, about 30 men, left behind in Lares by Rojas to defend the town against enemy attack, left their posts to join the priest in the Lares Church. Perhaps what the rebels did not know was that the priest, forced to perform the ceremony against his wishes, and frightened by the threats made against his life, would take revenge. According to Father Vega, he performed only a *Te Deum* pro-forma, dispensing with the most sacred rites necessary for such a glorious celebration.[67]

Having thanked God, albeit inappropriately, the rebel government returned to City Hall to await news from Rojas and to go on with the affairs of governing. But something had happened to them since attending Church. They had begun to question their actions.[68] Some of the men assigned to sentry duty abandoned their posts and went home. President Ramírez and the Minister of Justice, Clemente Millán, visited the prison to get ex-mayor Mediavilla to deliver the town's public funds, but failed to follow through. When they were told that the key to the town's money box was kept by Guillermo Frontera, they simply returned to City Hall, empty handed.[69] Perhaps once Rojas and the fighters left they felt exposed and alone. What they needed to recover their spirits was for Rojas' group to win over Pepino. With Cebollero and Ibarra, leaders of that town's militia, on their side, they were expected to capture the plaza and take over the weapons and munitions stored in the militia headquarters.[70] For those left back in Lares there was nothing else to do, but wait for the good news.

The Rebels Meet the Enemy at Pepino

News of Rojas and his rebel army approaching Pepino reached Manuel Cebollero and Eusebio Ibarra around eight the morning of the 24th.[71] Minutes later their joint forces of about 400 men, 50 of them on horses, were attacking the town.[72] They expected as Cebollero and Ibarra had promised the full cooperation of the militiamen under their command.[73] But what they found was a town ready for war.

The residents of Pepino, unlike those of Lares were wide awake and prepared to fight back. According to Jacinto García Pérez, the Corregidor of Aguadilla, he had come to investigate rumors of a rebel attack and had arrived in time to witness the real event.[74]

García Pérez reported that he had been discussing the rebels with the mayor of Pepino, Luis Chiesa, when he heard women screaming: "The revolutionaries, the Assassins are here," while doors were quickly being shut. At this point he stepped out onto the plaza revolver in hand, and came face to face with five or six men on horseback. They were screaming: "Death to the Spaniards, Death to the Queen, Long Live Free Puerto Rico." Incensed at such insults, García Pérez claimed to have ordered a rebel, aiming at him with a carbine, to give himself up in the name of the Queen. Instead, the rebel tried to shoot him, and had it not been for the night watchman of Pepino, Santiago Rodríguez, who jumped on the rebel, García Pérez would have probably been killed. Rodríguez' intervention, however, allowed García Pérez to shoot and wound the attacker.

Free of his assailant, García Pérez noticed that more rebels had entered the plaza. They were running up and down shooting and ordering the militiamen in the barracks to join them. García Pérez gave a counter order to shoot at the rebels, but found that they were already shooting. Civilians, too, were shooting from atop the houses and stores. They had all sorts of weapons, dynamite and gunpowder.

Yet the rebels kept coming. About 30 or 40 men, on horseback, kept shooting and giving orders to "kill the Spaniards." Among them were Cebollero and Ibarra urging the group to storm the barracks, and take the rifles and cartridges stored there. But reaching the barracks proved impossible. The militiamen inside were firing at them.[75] What had gone wrong? Cebollero and Ibarra tried to bring them back to their senses by shouting: "Milicianos, what are you doing?" But the men inside the barracks were no longer listening to their commands. They answered with more shots.[76]

After nearly half an hour of fighting, both groups retreated in order to regroup and attack once more. The rebels filed out, down Orejola Street, at the southern end of the plaza, and joined the rest of the rebel troops waiting on the other side of the bridge that separated the town from its rural countryside. Within minutes the rebels reappeared on the plaza. They were met by a heavy fusillade. Soon both sides suffered casualties. On the side of the rebels, three men were mortally wounded. One, Manuel de León, died within minutes, while Venancio Román, a militiaman from Lares, and another rebel from Mayagüez died during the next 24 hours.[77] Another rebel, Manuel Rosado Gimenez,[78] alias *el leñero*, received a wound in his right arm, from which he died in the jail of Aguadilla on 2 October. The loyalists Clement Borrero and Aniceto Ahorrio were also wounded in the skirmish.

The rebels retreated once more, but this time the loyalists followed them to the end of the plaza, chasing them up to the bridge. They could go no further, according to García Pérez, for fear of being defeated. Once the rebels had been routed, García Pérez decided it would be best for him to return to Aguadilla to send the Spanish military troops to protect the town.

On the other side of the bridge, Rojas discussed the idea of attacking once more, but several of his men opposed him.[79] They appeared to be confused by the hostile reception they received from the militiamen. They worried that if the corregidor of Aguadilla was already there the regular troops from Moca and Aguadilla were probably on their way.[80] They questioned their ability to withstand an armed confrontation with the Spanish troops, after having failed to secure the arsenal from Pepino. Finally, they reached the decision to return to Rojas' hacienda, where Matías Brugman was supposedly waiting for them with fresh troops from Mayagüez.[81]

The confrontation between rebels and loyalists had lasted no more than an hour. In that time six men had been wounded, four of them rebels, who eventually died, and two loyalists, who recovered. The battle at Pepino had been very different in nature from that of Lares. In Pepino, the residents had been warned two days before the attack that Ibarra and Cebollero had disappeared and that they were part of a plot to take over the town.

The mayor of Pepino, Luis Chiesa, had reported the rumors of the rebels' plans to the military commander of Aguadilla on 22 September. He had also requested troops to protect Pepino. While he waited for the commander's reply, he inspected the militia and placed its members under the command of Colonel Pedro Miguel San Antonio, a retired Spanish officer living in Pepino. San Antonio reviewed the troops, checked the weapons and munitions, and ordered the men to get ready for action. He also ordered the merchants in town to round up all the available gunpowder, and dynamite. Even "the pendulums of the clocks" were removed and stored for making cartridges.[82] Since the militiamen had come under suspicion, San Antonio confined them to the barracks, and armed civilians were placed on sentry duty outside the town.[83]

The Pepino confrontation ended with Rojas' decision to retreat to his hacienda. In the confusion that followed, Rojas left behind the wounded and seven prisoners, who were captured by the Spanish troops.[84] With the prisoners the rebels also lost nine horses and several weapons and cartridges. As he retreated, Rojas sent orders to the rebel government in Lares to take its prisoners and meet him at his hacienda.[85]

The courier, 16 year old Pablo Rivera y Delgado, reached Lares around noon and found three members of the Lares revolutionary government out to lunch in a nearby inn. Rivera called Francisco Ramírez aside and conveyed the message to move his men to Rojas' hacienda, as ordered.[86]

On the way to Rojas', Ramírez questioned the wisdom of Rojas' decision and ordered his men to free the prisoners. He arrived at Rojas' hacienda without the prisoners and without two members of his government. Aurelio Méndez and Federico Valencia had chosen to stay in Lares, despite Rojas' orders to the contrary.[87]

Why Rojas called the rebels to his hacienda that afternoon is still unclear since none of those captured admitted having been there, for fear of being linked to the attack on Pepino.[88] We have no way of knowing if Rojas planned to continue fighting once he met with Matías Brugman. Nor do we have any evidence to substantiate Pérez Moris' claim that Brugman and Rojas argued over the decision to retreat from Pepino. We can only speculate, on the basis of data obtained from some witnesses,[89] that their ultimate decision must have been to retreat into the hills and avoid being captured. Perhaps the leaders entertained the idea that their retreat would be for a few days, until Betances and his men reached them on the 29th of September, as planned. But, having made the decision to stop fighting they surrendered the stage to the Spanish authorities and thus ceased to be in command. The fact that no other town seconded the cry of Lares, and that Betances was not able to reach Puerto Rico[90] brought the uprising to its end. Without ships in which to escape from the island, and without aid from the outside, the rebels had no choice but to take to the hills. It would be a matter of time before the colonial officials would have them behind bars. The government had given orders to implement the skillfully designed counterinsurgency plan of Sabino Gamir y Maladeñ, which recommended, among other things, blocking the rebels' exit to the sea.

NOTES

1   See the report sent by Iturriaga to Governor Julián Juan Pavía, 19 December 1868, in AGPR, FGEPR, *La Revolución de Lares 1868*, Caja 180, Pieza 43, f. 75.

2   See Castañón's testimony, given to Judge Navascués, 19 December 1868, in AGPR, FGEPR, *La Revolución de Lares 1868*, Caja 181, Pieza 47, 48, ff. 77, 78 (hereafter cited as Castañón Testimony, 19 December 1868).

3   Castañón Testimony, Ibid., f. 78.

4   Castañón Testimony, Ibid.

5   Until 1832, when the Puerto Rican Audiencia was first established, there were innumerable cases of trespassing by the military authorities. The civilian courts complained repeatedly and the Crown sought to correct the problem by creating this High Court. For Castañón's decisions, see his testimony, Ibid.

6   Testimony of Juan Castañón, Arecibo, 30 December 1868, in AGPR, FGEPR, *La Revolución de Lares 1868*, Caja 180, Pieza 43 (hereafter cited as Castañón, Second Testimony).

7   Testimony of Francisco Alcazar, Arecibo, 18 December 1868, in AGPR, FGEPR, *La Revolución de Lares 1868*, Caja 180, Pieza 43, f. 75.

8   Alcazar's Testimony, Ibid.

9   Alcazar's Testimony, Ibid.

10   Castañón Testimony, 19 December 1868, f. 18.

11   *Oficio* sent by Iturriaga to Governor Julián J. Pavía, the night of 20 September 1868, in AGPR, FGEPR, *La Revolución de Lares 1868*, Caja 180, Pieza 43, f. 75; also in Juan Castañón Testimony, Ibid.

12   In the testimonies of Ramón Estrella, Bartolomé González Soto, José Antonio Hernández and several others, in AGPR, FGEPR, *La Revolución de Lares 1868*, Caja 178, Pieza 13.

13   Manuel María González, contrary to what is believed, did not reveal any information about the conspiracy until 20 October. By that time Judge Navascués had much information from other members, particularly from José Antonio Hernández, a member of Lanzador del Norte, who on 25 September took the troops under Iturriaga to the place on his farm where the cartridges for the revolution had been hidden. In AGPR, FGEPR, *La Revolución de Lares 1868*, Caja 178, Pieza 13.

14   Based on documents that were sent by Governor Pavía to the Overseas Minister in Madrid which appear in A.H.N., Madrid, "Documentos . . . Sublevación de Lares," Exp. 20128, Doc. 17, p. 34.

15   Ibid.

16   According to Iturriaga, *Oficio*, 20 September 1868, in AGPR, FGEPR, *La Revolución de Lares 1868*, Caja 180, P. 43, f. 75.

17   In the Testimony of Ramón Estrella, one of the members present at Carlos Martínez' house, in AGPR, FGEPR, *La Revolución de Lares 1868*, Caja 178, Pieza 13.

18   Testimony of José Antonio Hernández, Arecibo, 24-25 September 1868, in AGPR, FGEPR, *La Revolución de Lares 1868*, Caja 178, Pieza 13.

19   Hernández' reluctance to follow Carlos Martínez and the latter's threat on his life was corroborated by several jornaleros working for Hernández.

20   *Oficio* from Iturriaga to Governor Julián Juan Pavía, discussed in José Pérez Moris, *Historia de la Insurrección de Lares*, p. 120.

21   Reported by Judge Navascués in his *Informe Final*, p. 6. Also see the Testimony of Ramón Estrella, Arecibo, 4 November 1868, in AGPR, FGEPR, *La Revolución de Lares 1868*, Caja 178, Pieza 13.

22   What went on in Brugman's house was told to Judge Navascués by a member of Capá Prieto, Juan Vicentí, in his Testimony, Arecibo, 29 October 1868, in AGPR, FGEPR, *La Revolución de Lares 1868*, Caja 180, Pieza 13.

23   According to Vicentí, those present at the meeting of 22 September were: Matías Brugman's son, Enrique; Matias' son-in-law Agustín Lara, also his step-son, José Antonio Muse, alias Garzón, two of the brothers Beauchamp, Dionisio and Elías; the two Arroyo brothers, Juan de Mata Terreforte, Bruno Chabrier, Pedro (Pepe) García (a Dominican, who worked for Brugman), and Juan Vicentí. He added that there were others he could not remember. In Vincentí's Testimony of 29 October, Ibid.

24   Based on the Testimony of Eugenio Bernard, given in Mayagüez on 2 October 1868, in AGPR, FGEPR, *La Revolución de Lares 1868*, Caja 177, Pieza 11. Eugenio Bernard was born in Isabela, but lived in barrio Furnias #2, Mayagüez. He was listed as an hacendado, owner of the slave Juan Pío. For details about Bernard, see in AGPR, FGEPR, *La Revolución de Lares 1868*, Caja 181, Piezas 47, 48.

25   This information is based on the Testimony of José Capestane, in Aguadilla, 15 January 1869, which appears in AGPR, FGEPR, *La Revolución de Laries 1868*, Caja 179, Pieza 40.

26   Testimony given by Caloca before Judge Navascués, Lares, 19 October 1868, in AGPR, FGEPR, *La Revolución de Lares 1868*, Caja 178, Pieza 12.

27   Based on conversations Pérez Moris had with several members of the Lares community after the uprising was defeated. In his book, *Historia de la Insurrección de Lares*, p. 136.

28   Testimony of Eugenio Bernard, Mayagüez, 2 October 1868, in AGPR, FGEPR, *La Revolución de Lares 1868*, Caja 177, Pieza 11.

29   Many of the slaves present at Chabrier's and Brugman's haciendas that morning later testified that they had taken part in the Lares revolt by order of their masters, who promised them their freedom in exchange for their support. One example of this type of testimony is that given by Polinario, slave of José Antonio Muse, on 25 September in Mayagüez. Copy of his testimony, and those of several others, appears in AGPR, FGEPR, *La Revolución de Lares 1868*, Caja 177, Pieza 22 (25-29 September).

30   According to Cándido (alias Yuyú, a 25 year old slave who belonged to Pedro Beauchamp, present at Chabrier's hacienda the morning of 23 September 1868, he and Pascasio, another slave who belonged to Pablo Beauchamp, had intimidated

a number of jornaleros working for Juan Mata Dumó, forcing them to join the rebel forces. In AGPR, FGEPR, *La Revolución de Lares 1868*, Caja 177, Pieza 11.

31   Based on the Testimony of Polinario, Mayagüez, 25 September 1868, in AGPR, FGEPR, *La Revolución de Lares 1868*, Caja 177, Pieza 11.

32   For the testimonies of the men who claimed to have been coerced into joining the rebels of Mayagüez, see the interrogations of Pedro Mata Ríos, Pedro Ríos Alicea and others, Mayagüez, 28 September 1868, in Ibid., Caja 177, Pieza 11.

33   See the correspondence between Governor Julián Juan Pavía, the Justices of the Peace of Mayagüez, Aguadilla, Ponce and Arecibo, and the Real Audiencia, in AGPR, FGEPR, *La Revolución de Lares 1868*, Caja 176, Piezas 2, 3, and in Ibid., Caja 177, Piezas 11, 12.

34   Among those who followed their employers to Lares was Maximiliano Sánchez, a jornalero who worked for don Pedro Pablo González, in Aguada. He gave a list of about 15 others who followed don Pedro Pablo to Lares. For his testimony, see in AGPR, FGEPR, *La Revolución de Lares 1868*, Aguadilla, 20 January 1869, Caja 180, Pieza 42.

35   The estimate is based on testimonies of persons later arrested. This figure also corresponds to that given by the peasant farmer accompanying them, Antonio Ruperto Rondón. See his testimony, given in Aguadilla, 18 January 1869, in AGPR, FGEPR, *La Revolución de Lares 1868*, Caja 179, Pieza 41.

36   According to the slave Victorio (owned by José Antonio Muse), the trip from Buena Vista to Pezuela, including their many stops, took nearly four hours. See his testimony, Aguadilla, January 1869, in AGPR, FGEPR, *La Revolución de Lares 1868*, Caja 180, Pieza 43; also testimony of Pedro Ríos Alicea, Mayagüez, 28 September 1868, in Ibid., Caja 177, Pieza 11.

37   Testimony of the slave Santana (owned by Eugenio Bernard), Arecibo, 31 December 1868, in *Boletín de Historia Puertorriqueña*, Vol. II, No. 6 (Mayo 1950), pp. 177-178.

38   Cited by the slave Polinario (owned by José Antonio Muse), in his testimony of 25 September 1868, in AGPR, FGEPR, *La Revolución de Lares 1868*, Caja 177, Pieza 11.

39   Based on Judge Navascués *Informe Final*, p. 7.

40   Navascués *Informe Final*, p. 7.

41   Based on the testimony of Maximiliano Sánchez, Aguadilla, 20 January 1869, in AGPR, FGEPR, *La Revolución de Lares 1868*, Caja 180, Pieza 42.

42   None of the 20 jornaleros interrogated by Judge Navascués claimed to have been forced by Pedro Pablo González' troops. They claimed instead that they did not know the purpose of their trip to Lares. See the testimony of Juan Cruz Alicea, Aguadilla, 20 January 1868, in Ibid.

43   Testimony of Juan Paz Rosado, Aguadilla, 20 January 1868, in AGPR, FGEPR, *La Revolución de Lares 1868*, Caja 180, Pieza 42; also in Navascués *Informe Final*, p. 7.

44   The dress of Rojas was described in José Antonio Muse's testimony, Aguadilla, January 1869, Ibid., Caja 180, Pieza 43.

45   Navascués *Informe Final*, p. 7; also Muse's Testimony, Ibid.

46   Based on documents found in A.H.N., Madrid, "Documentos . . . Sublevación de Lares," Exp. 20128, Doc. 24.

47   The exact number of rebels who left Rojas' hacienda is not known. Estimates range from 600 to 1,000. We are accepting the lower estimate given by José Antonio Muse, because it corresponds fairly closely to the number of persons who were later accused by other members of the rebel group.

48   José Antonio Muse stated that between Rojas' hacienda and the town of Lares there had been "great destruction." Also in Navascués *Informe Final*, p. 8.

49   Navascués, *Informe Final*, p. 8.

50   According to the testimony of the Mayor of Lares, in AGPR, FGEPR, *La Revolución de Lares 1868*, Caja 178, Pieza 12 (Aguadilla, 19 October 1868).

51   Navascués *Informe Final*, p. 9.

52   According to Caloca's story, which is retold in Navascues' *Informe Final*, p. 9.

53   Pérez Moris, *Historia de la Insurrección de Lares*, p. 136.

54   See the descriptions of the weapons and the town's takeover by Fidel Navas, *Boletín de Historia Puertorriqueña*, Vol. II, No. 5 (Abril 1950), p. 149.

55   Fidel Navas' Testimony, Ibid.

56   It appears that Carlos Feliciano was accidentally shot by one of his own men; Navas' Testimony, Ibid.

57   According to the testimony of Tomás Valentín, a jornalero on the lands of Ferrer, given in Aguadilla, 19 October 1868, in AGPR, FGEPR, *La Revolución de Lares 1868*, Caja 178, Pieza 12.

58   According to García Pérez, the damages caused by the rebels mounted to 20,000 pesos. The estimate included the cheese, crackers, and liquor the rebels consumed, as well as the weapons, gunpowder, cartridges, clothes, and horses the rebels confiscated. In AGPR, FGEPR, *La Revolución de Lares 1868*, Caja 178, Pieza 12.

59   Based on testimony of Francicso Ramírez, given in Aguadilla, 7 January 1869, in *Boletín de Historia Puertorriqueña*, Vol. II, No. 6 (Mayo 1950), pp. 196-201.

60   Navascués, *Informe Final*, p. 11.

61   Testimony of Francisco Ramírez, Aguadilla, 7 January 1869, in *Boletín de Historia Puertorriqneña*, Ibid., p. 197.

62   Francisco Ramírez' Testimony, Ibid.

63   Documents taken by the military troops and presented to Bernabé Pol by the judge during the interrogations. Bernabé Pol recognized these and other circulars posted by his men the night of 23 September. For details on this interrogation, see in AGPR, *Audiencia Territorial, Tribunal Pleno*, Caja 7, Pieza I, ff. 19-22.

64   The document was presented to Ramírez, by Judge Navascués on 7 January 1869. Ramírez admitted having written the document, which appears in AGPR, *Audiencia Territorial, Tribunal Pleno*, Caja 7, Pieza I, f. 18.

65   Document found in AGPR, *Audiencia Territorial, Tribunal Pleno*, Caja 7, Pieza I, f. 18.

66   Aurelio Méndez, in his testimony, Arecibo, 1 October 1868, in AGPR, FGEPR, *La Revolución de Lares 1868*, Caja 178, Pieza 13.

67   Based on the explanations given by Father Vega to his superior, the Bishop of San Juan, his letters are in AGPR, *Audiencia Territorial, Tribunal Pleno*, Caja 7, Pieza 1, pp. 36-39.

68   Based on the testimonies of several men who served as guards of Lares the night of the 23rd and the morning of the 24th. See the statements made by Pedro Giménes, Arecibo, 4 October 1868, in AGPR, FGEPR, *La Revolución de Lares 1868*, Caja 178, Pieza 13; Juan Arroyo Pedrosa, Arecibo, 4 October 1868, Ibid.; and Pedro Román, Arecibo, 4 October 1868, Ibid.

69   Based on the testimony of Pablo Mediavilla, given in Aguadilla, 19 October 1868, in AGPR, FGEPR, *La Revolución de Lares 1868*, Caja 178, Pieza 12.

70   Testimonies of Francisco Ramírez and Clemente Millán, Aguadilla, 7 January 1869. In *Boletín de Historia Puertorriqueña*, Vol. II, No. 7 (Junio 1950), pp. 196-201.

71 Based on the testimonies of Eusebio Ibarra, Lares, 8 October 1868, in AGPR, *Audiencia Territorial, Tribunal Pleno*, Caja 7, Pieza I, p. 54; Manuel Cebollero, Yauco, 8 October 1868, in AGPR, FGEPR, *La Revolución de Lares 1868*, Caja 177, Pieza 11.

72 Based on Cebollero's testimony and on the official report submitted by the Corregidor of Aguadilla, Jacinto Barcía Pérez, to Governor Julián Juan Pavía, on 24 September 1868, which appears in AGPR, *Audiencia Territorial, Tribunal Pleno*, Caja 7, Pieza I, pp. 7-10.

73 Based on the testimony of a Spaniard, Manuel Bernal, who was assigned to keep the militiamen in Pepino from joining the rebels. His testimony appears in *Boletín de Historia Puertorriqueña*, Vol. II, No. 5 (Abril 1950), pp. 131-132.

74 García Pérez, Report, 24 September 1868.

75 Testimony of Manuel Bernal, in *Boletín de Historia Puertorriqueña*, Ibid.

76 Testimony of Manuel Bernal, in *Boletín de Historia Puertorriqueña*, Ibid.

77 In the testimony of Gabriel Socias, in *Boletín de Historia Puertorriqueña*, Vol. II, No. 5 (Abril 1950), pp. 133-134.

78 His participation in the Pepino attack, his death in Aguadilla, and his nickname were found in AGPR, FGEPR, *La Revolución de Lares 1868*, Caja 181, Piezas 47, 48.

79 Based on the testimony of Pedro Ríos, one of the rebels on the outskirts of Pepino that morning, given in Aguadilla, 7 January 1869, in *Boletín de Historia Puertorriqueña*, Vol. II, No. 7 (Junio 1950), p. 201.

80 According to the story told by Juan de Mata Terreforte, Aguadilla, 23 December 1868, in *Boletín de Historia Puertorriqueña*, Vol. II, No. 6 (Mayo 1950), p. 163.

81 Based on the testimony of José García Berenguer, a schoolteacher, resident of Mayagüez, who accompanied the rebels as a leader the morning of the 24th. His testimony was given in Arecibo, 15 October 1868 and appears in AGPR, FGEPR, *La Revolución de Lares 1868*, Caja 178, Pieza 12.

82 This is part of a report Mayor Chiesa showed García Pérez the morning of the 24th. Reported by García Pérez to the Governor of Puerto Rico, 2 October 1868, in AGPR, *Audiencia Territorial, Tribunal Pleno*, Caja 7, Pieza I, pp. 41-42.

83 Told by Manuel Bernal in his testimony, in *Boletín de Historia Puertorriqueña*, Vol. II, No. 5 (Abril 1950), pp. 130-131.

84 Judge Tomás de Morales to Audiencia on 29 September 1868, which appears in AGPR, *Audiencia Territorial, Tribunal Pleno*, Caja 7, Pieza I, pp. 18-23.

85 Ibid.

86 See the testimony of Fidel Navas in *Boletín de Historia Puertorriqueña*, Vol. II, No. 5 (Abril 1950), p. 150. See Médez' testimony, Arecibo, 1 October 1868, AGPR, FGEPR, *La Revolución de Lares 1868*, Caja 178, Pieza 13.

87 Francisco Ramírez, Testimony, Aguadilla, 7 January 1869, in *Boletín de Historia Puertorriqueña*, Vol. II, no. 7 (Junio 1950).

88 Based on the circular sent by Governor Pavía to the district military commanders on 27 September 1868, the military courts were entitled to try and sentence any person caught with weapons in his/her possession, found to be resisting the troops. See Pavía's Circular of 27 September 1868, in AGPR, *Audiencia Territorial, Tribunal Pleno*, Caja 7, Pieza I, pp. 16-17.

89 See Manuel Ramírez' Testimony, Aguadilla, 26 January 1869, in AGPR, FGEPR, *La Revolución de Lares 1868*, Caja 180, Pieza 42. Also see Aurelio Méndez' testimony of 11 October 1868, Aguadilla, in Ibid., Caja 178, Pieza 13.

90. According to Lidio Cruz Monclova, Betances and his men were kept from leaving Santo Domingo by order of the president, Buenaventura Báez. Saint Thomas confiscated the rebels' ship, *El Telégrafo*. In Cruz Monclova, *Historia*, I, p. 450.

V
Capture and Imprisonment of the Rebels

On the afternoon of 24 September Manuel Rojas in Lares debated with his men whether to continue fighting or to take refuge in the hills until some other town seconded their struggle. That same day Governor Julián Juan Pavía in San Juan gave orders to Lieutenant Colonel Sabino Gamir y Maladeñ to go immediately to Arecibo to investigate the conspiracy reported by the Corregidor Manuel de Iturriaga.[1] Governor Pavía, who did not yet know about the attack against Lares merely sent Gamir on a routine investigation. Thus, he instructed Gamir to meet with the commander of Arecibo and the mayor of Camuy before taking command of the military troops there. Once in command, if in fact peace was threatened, he was to order (the rebels) to disband. But if they refused, he was to disband them by force, with the armed men at his disposal.[2]

Before Colonel Gamir reached Arecibo, a sea-journey that took him nearly 24 hours, Governor Pavía received news of the attack against Lares and Pepino and had to change his strategy and proceed with a counter-revolutionary attack.[3]

The Gamir Plan in Operation

On the evening of 25 September, he put into operation the counter-insurgency plan Colonel Gamir had drafted two years before.[4] After issuing orders to the district military commanders to dispatch troops to Lares, Pavía ordered the military commander of San Juan, Colonel J. Manuel de Ibarreta, to move three companies from the Cadiz Batallion to cover the ports of Arecibo and Aguadilla immediately.[5] Ibarretta sailed that very evening on the war ship *Vasco Nuñez de Balboa* with instructions to dispatch his columns from different points on the island to close in on the rebels who tried to reach the ports.[6]

News of the attack on Lares and Pepino reached the military commanders of Ponce and Mayagüez before they reached the government in San Juan. The commander of Mayagüez, Colonel Antonio de Balboa, was among the first to dispatch a column to the troubled area on 24 September. That same afternoon he ordered Lieutenant José de Arce, of the Valladolid Battalion to

97

organize a search expedition and proceed to Pepino and Lares. Arce was instructed to take his party through Las Marías, a densely wooded area which could serve as a hideout to the fleeing rebels. He reached Pepino the next morning without encountering the insurgents.[7] In Pepino, Arce took command of the town's military operations, ordering 60 militiamen to protect the area while he continued his trip to Lares.[8] Meanwhile in Arecibo, Colonel Iturriaga received from his troops on Camuy a list of suspects hiding in the surrounding barrios. By the evening of the 24th the Arecibo troops, led by Captain José Pujol, brought in the rebel member of Lanzador del Norte, José Antonio Hernández.[9] Interrogated by Iturriaga that evening, Hernández at first resisted talking, but after several hours in solitary confinement, told everything he knew.[10] Thus by the time Colonel Gamir reached Arecibo on 25 September, Iturriaga had concrete news to give him. As evidence, he had two boxes containing about 1,000 dynamite sticks and a sack of gunpowder Hernández had buried in his farm, in barrio Piedra Gorda.[11]

On the morning of the 26th Pavía's second representative, Colonel J. Manuel de Ibarreta also stopped in Arecibo to assign one of the columns to patrol the port. With Gamir and Iturriaga covering the Arecibo district, he pushed on to Aguadilla with over 100 armed men he was given in Arecibo.[12] He too converged on Pepino the evening of the 26th. After a day's rest in Pepino, Ibarreta took his troops to Lares. There he received instructions from Governor Pavía to take command of the entire military operation connected to the Lares affair.[13]

From Bayamón (part of the San Juan district), two additional columns were dispatched on 27 September under the command of Pedro Resano. Like all other columns, those of Bayamón were to make their way to Lares. Following a southwesterly direction they searched the towns of Toa Alta, Corozal, Morovis, Ciales, Utuado, reaching Lares on October 1st. In Lares, Resano was named commander of the *Columna de Observación de Lares*, which, including his own men, amounted to 339 men, 11 of them officers.[14]

From Ponce two columns were dispatched to Adjuntas. One of them left on the 26th, under Sergeant Iglesias. The other left the next morning headed by Colonel Francisco Martínez. Each column consisted of 85 military men 20 of whom were from the cavalry division.[15] It was the last column to leave Ponce that captured the first rebel leaders.[16]

According to a report of the column's commander, Colonel Martínez, he had advance information that some rebels were hiding in the area of Adjuntas. Thus, he secured the aid of two guides and searched the barrios of Guilarte, Limani and Guayo. The *comisario* of barrio Guayo, José Aparicio, confirmed the rumors about rebels hiding nearby and offered his help to search the hacienda of Eduardo Quiñones. Two rebel leaders were said to be hiding[17] there with the cooperation of the comisario of Rio Prieto, Bernardo Navarro.[18]

Martínez reached Quiñones' hacienda about 5:30 in the afternoon of the thirtieth and ordered Lieutenant Costa to search the place while he waited for the comisario Navarro, who was expected shortly. Navarro arrived soon after, saying that everything was in order, that there were no strangers in the area.[19] Just then Lieutenant Costa emerged from Quiñones' house with three men and a number of weapons he had found on the premises.[20] Questioned separately, each of the men said the weapons belonged to the comisario, who as an officer of the law was entitled to them. But Colonel Martínez was still suspicious of Navarro and decided interrogate him about the weapons. He reported what took place as follows:

When I asked him to identify each weapon . . . he became confused, so I threatened him severely, telling him that this would be the last minute of his life unless he told me how many rebels were there and where they were hiding.[21]

According to Colonel Martínez, his threats frightened Navarro so much that he not only told him there were two rebels in the coffee grove, but also suggested the surest way to capture them. Martínez stated in his report:

Once we reached the place I deliberated about the best way to capture them before they had a chance to escape. Navarro told me that the best way was to have his worker, the old man Francisco Quiñones, lead the way.[22]

Summoning Quiñones at once, Martínez threatened him with the loss of his life unless he cooperated and led them to the rebels' hideout. After a five hour march Martínez and three of his men fell upon the rebels Matías Brugman and Baldomero (Guayubin) Bauring, who were sleeping at the base of a tree, in the middle of the grove. Martínez reported:

. . . when we fell upon them we woke them with our noise; they grabbed their revolvers and fired, missing us. We fired, killing them instantly. One I hit in the head. The other was killed by one of my men.[23]

He also reported that two other prisoners had been captured by the men guarding the rear. One, named Bautista Toledo, had been seriously wounded while trying to escape.[24]

In Camuy, Colonel Sabino Gamir had arrested some 20 suspects.[25] But in the Lares-Pepino area the military operations were less successful. Suspecting that the rebels were already hiding in the sierra of the western interior, Colonel Ibarreta moved most of his troops from Lares and Pepino to the mountains of the interior. He assigned these troops to Sierra Alta, and Indiera

and those of Ponce (commanded by Martínez, Iglesias, and Prats) to patrol
the Adjuntas-Maricao area. Colonel Gamir and his men were taken from
Camuy to Mayagüez where they were to search Brugman's house and to
patrol the area surrounding the hacienda.

With the concentration of troops, moving in from several directions, the
rebels hiding in the area of Sierra Alta had little chance to escape. It would
be a question of time before they were captured and put behind bars. By the
morning of 2 October the combined forces of Colonel Martínez and Captain
Prats arrested the hacendados Ernesto and Leopoldo Nigaglioni and the
fugitives Leoncio Rivera and Pedro Segundo García.[26] The same afternoon,
they also captured Francisco Ramírez, Andrés Pol, Manuel Rojas, Manuel
Cebollero, Rudolfo Echevarría, and Clemente Millán. In just one day the
troops had captured 10 important rebels, four of whom had formed part of
the provisional revolutionary government. One had been the commanding
general of the rebel army, and another had led the rebel troops to Pepino.

It was later told by a soldier in Colonel Martínez' camp that Manuel Rojas
had been subjected to great abuse by his captors. He said:

> (Once) captured Rojas was, by (order of Martínez), hung by his hands
> from one of the beams of the house where he was found hiding. In that
> suspended position, in the presence of all the soldiers, he (Martínez)
> slapped and spat on his face. He hit him with his revolver in the mouth
> until it was all bloody. He pulled his beard so hard that part of it ended in
> his hand, with some flesh still attached to it.[27]

In addition to the rebels, the Ponce troops also captured 12 horses with
their saddles, a sack full of gunpowder and many cartridges and bullets. For
this work, the Martínez-Prats company was effusively congratulated by Governor Pavía on 7 October.[28]

The arrests continued even though the governor was growing weary of the
whole affair. In Mayagüez, a column commanded by Cayetano Iborti captured in barrio Guabas, the rebel Telesforo Angleró. Also in Mayagüez
Colonel Gamir arrested the hacendados Enrique Brugman and Eugenio and
Bruno Chabrier.

The jails of the western region appeared to be bursting with prisoners.
This fact, added to the latest report from Martínez reporting the capture of
so many rebel leaders, led the Governor to conclude that it was time to end
the military expedition. But first he had to reassure the inhabitants that the
event in Lares was over and the island was no longer in danger. He asked them
to forget the event, that he would make sure that no one escaped the conse-
quences of this criminal act.[29]

Soon after the Governor gave his speech, many members of the municipal
juntas sent congratulatory letters approving his swift end to the uprising.[30]

Some members wrote personal letters pledging to "sacrifice life and estate" to bring the island back to its "usual tranquility."[31]

In Ponce, the governor's speech prompted the military commander, Eliseo Berriz, to issue a circular to reassure the inhabitants.[32] He explained that these assurances were necessary because the inhabitants had just learned that Ponce was the place where the rebel leaders were to be tried by a War Council.

On 10 October, Governor Pavía reported to the Overseas Minister in Madrid that with the capture of all (the rebels), particularly the Venezuelan Manuel Rojas, the Lares rebellion was over. He downplayed the number of prisoners, stating that there were about 200.[33]

During the third week of October the troops of Pedro Resano in Lares and Luis Prats in Yauco captured a few other insurgents still at large. In Lares Resano apprehended Gabino Plumey, Santiago Casas, Manuel Ramírez and Ignacio Balbino Ostolaza the morning of the 16th. Since the Lares jail was overflowing, Resano sent the new prisoners, along with Eusebio Ibarra, arrested eight days earlier to the district jail of Aguadilla. Two days later in Yauco Captain Prats reported having shot to death the rebel Joaquín Parrilla.[34]

By mid-October the jails of Ponce, Arecibo, Aguadilla and Lares were so full that private quarters had to be rented to house the incoming prisoners.[35] Everyone, including the Governor, was anxious to get on with the investigation, to punish the guilty and free the others.[36] He had become extremely worried about the growing number of prisoners in the overcrowded jails. Over 500 men had been imprisoned in less than one month. He feared for their lives, as epidemics broke out in several jails, and worried about the economic burden the troops caused to the island's treasury. Thus he decided to disband the troops and let the courts do their work. But as he prepared to remove the troops, he received news from Madrid that Spain itself was undergoing a revolution. Fearing that Spain's upheaval might encourage more revolts on the island, he decided to wait, while at the same time urging the troops to remain calm. He reminded them that no matter what happened in Spain "your mission here (Puerto Rico) is to protect the interests of the patria."[37]

Finally, on 24 October he ordered the active military troops to return to their headquarters and the reserve troops to disband at once. He explained to the military commanders that except for a few fugitives who were still at large all other rebels had been apprehended. He urged them "to return to the(ir) headquarters to enjoy a well-deserved rest and the compliments they had earned." He cautioned that it was time to lighten the load on the treasury.[38]

What the Governor did not say, but which also influenced his decision were the facts that over 40 prisoners had already died in jail and that 14 days before Cuba had declared war against Spain. The Governor feared that if conditions in Puerto Rico were not stabilized soon they could provoke an invasion by the Cuban and Puerto Rican rebels in exile.[39] He believed, as did the governor before him, that the island lacked the men and resources to defeat a revolt with outside support. Time, however, would prove that his biggest problem would be to make the civil and military courts cooperate with one another.

The Judicial Process

Four days after the revolt of Lares Governor Pavía mobilized the armed forces. Having activated the military, a question arose immediately as to which branch of colonial justice would try the rebels once they were captured.[40] The old squabble between the civil and the military branches of government was re-kindled when on 28 September Governor Pavía handed the investigation to Audiencia. He gave the civil court jurisdiction over "all the rebels apprehended in connection with Lares, except those carrying weapons [at the time of the arrest] and those who resisted the authorities."[41] On the 29th, he specifically asked the Regent of Audiencia, Andrés Avelino de Mena, to take the necessary steps to set up a court of justice in the immediate area of the uprising.[42] It was made clear to the Regent that the judge appointed by Audiencia and the special court it created would be in charge of the investigation.

Audiencia moved quickly, appointing on 29 September the district judge of Ponce, Nicasio de Navascués y Aisa, to head the Lares investigation.[43] It then also explained to the other district judges that the nature and seriousness of the crimes committed required that the proceedings be centralized under one judge.[44] To Judge Navascués the orders were to hand over his duties as district judge of Ponce to a qualified person and move to Arecibo where he was to set up a special court to deal with the rebels involved in the uprising.[45] Audiencia also advised him to take along the attorney general and the scribe under his command in Ponce to help him set up the new court.

On 2 October, Navascués boarded the ship *Aguila* with the persons who would constitute his court.[46] He would travel to Arecibo via the ports of Mayagüez and Aguadilla,[47] to claim from those districts the prisoners that now belonged to his jurisdiction. He stopped briefly in Mayagüez to take charge of 30 prisoners and several weapons being guarded by the corregidor.

Bad weather and poor roads forced Navascués to continue his trip aboard the Aguila, delaying his arrival to Aguadilla until the afternoon of 3 October. Among the 52 prisoners that Aguadilla placed under his jurisdiction were a brother of Joaquín Parrilla and two brothers of Manuel Rojas.[48] Having claimed these prisoners, he had to leave them in the same jails because Arecibo did not have adequate space for all of them.

Traveling by night to save time, Navascués finally reached Arecibo the morning of 4 October. After setting up his court, he went to claim the prisoners under Corregidor Iturriaga's custody.[49]

From Arecibo Navascués complained to Audiencia about the inadequate space in the jails, the lack of personnel, and the cramped, unsanitary conditions that prevailed in the prisons. He explained that such conditions made it impossible to keep the prisoners incommunicado and threatened the lives of the inmates. Yellow fever he said had already claimed several lives. He would complain about these problems repeatedly during the next few months.

Navascués remained in Arecibo until the night of 5 October, when he resumed his journey to Lares. He complained to Audiencia that there were so many tasks to occupy him such as interrogating prisoners by day, writing reports to Audiencia, and traveling by night that he hardly had time for sleep.[50]

The bad conditions of the dirt roads were made worse by that evening's rains. Flooded rivers along the way made certain stretches hazardous, making the 21 miles between Arecibo and Lares into a grueling journey of 11 hours.[51] Without sleep and "burning with fever", Navascués opened his court in Lares the morning of 6 October. For four days he worked frantically, taking testimonies of over 100 prisoners, ordering dozens of arrests and reading the certified depositions made by the rebel leader Eusebio Ibarra. Ibarra's testimony provided the names of many persons who were later arrested.[52]

The arrival of new prisoners to the jails of Aguadilla and Mayagüez forced Navascués to return to Arecibo after only one week in Lares. He explained to Audiencia that there was no way he could keep traveling between one jail and the other while his affairs went unattended in Arecibo. Thus, he suggested that the scattered prisoners be taken to San Juan, the only place capable of housing all of them within a small geographical area.[53]

Governor Pavía quickly rejected Navascués' request, stating that such a measure would be counter productive since it would excite the residents of the capital and make visitors curious about the stability of the Spanish Government in Puerto Rico. Fearing that such a move would bring unwanted publicity, Pavía suggested that the prisoners be kept where they were and that the judge expedite the legal proceedings to allow the innocent to get back to work as soon as possible.[54]

The Governor's refusal was accompanied by a new set of instructions from Audiencia which allowed a more active role to the military court against the rebels. The new instructions, as drafted by the Auditor of War, stated that any person who had taken part in the attack against Pepino had in effect resisted the authorities and should be turned over to the War Council (in Ponce). Contrary to Pavía's earlier instructions, the Auditor explained that it was unimportant whether or not the rebels were carrying weapons when apprehended. He added that the mere fact that they did not resist the troops at the time of arrest did not mean that they had not done so previously in Pepino. Thus, he concluded that Navascués' duty was to determine which prisoners had taken part in the attack against Pepino and turn them over to the War Council without further delay.[55]

By requesting the intervention of the Auditor of War, Governor Pavía was trying to ease the tensions that were growing between the civil and military courts.[56] He had been made aware that his decision to hand over the investigation to the civil court had antagonized the military and thus threatened to delay the proceedings unnecessarily.

A letter from Navascués on 1 October illustrates the stalling tactics used by the military authorities. He complained to Audiencia that the corregidor of Mayagüez had violated the Governor's instructions of 28 September by placing under military jurisdiction a man suspected of having taken part in the attack of Lares even though the suspect had voluntarily turned himself in. Navascués reminded Audiencia that such a prisoner belonged to the civil court since he had not resisted arrest nor was found to have been carrying weapons at the time of arrest. At the same time Governor Pavía heard many complaints from the military officers in the field. They complained that by the time they apprehended their suspects these had gotten rid of their weapons and made no attempt to resist arrest. Thus, they wondered how they were to obtain the prisoners that were to be tried by the military courts. It was this dilemma that led Pavía to seek help from the Auditor of War and to follow his instructions after 15 October. But despite the new instructions, his failing health, and the pressures placed by the governor, Navascués would not relinquish his court's right to claim all prisoners. He obeyed orders insofar as he adopted the shorter and sharply focused questionnaire provided by Audiencia. But he no longer tried to isolate the prisoners and often took their depositions within earshot of one another. As a result, the suspects made up stories and covered up each other, making it difficult for the courts to determine if they had in fact resisted the authorities at Pepino.

Meanwhile, the War Council clamored for its right to bring the rebels to justice and several hacendados petitioned the release of the workers. Frustrated by the judge's stubbornness, Governor Pavía decided to appeal to the Regent of Audiencia.[57] On 4 November he asked the Regent to restrain Navascués from further interference with rebel leaders who had taken part in the attack against Pepino. Without naming them, Pavía was referring to the nine men captured by Colonel Martínez who were then being held by the military authorities of Ponce. The Regent complied at once with Pavía's petition and the way was finally cleared for the military court to dispense its own justice. By 17 November seven of the nine rebel leaders had been tried and sentenced to death by the War Council. Sentenced to death by the *garrote* were: Clodomiro Euclides Abril, Rodulfo Echevarría, Pedro S. García, Ignacio Balbino Ostolaza, Andrés Pol, Leoncio Rivera, and Manuel Rojas.[58] The military sentences were quickly signed by Governor Pavía on 21 November.[59]

Despite the swiftness with which the military court tried the rebels, the death sentences were never carried out. Just six days after he signed their death sentences Governor Pavía commuted five of them, ordering instead that they serve 10 years in prison, anywhere in Spain. The two whose sentences were left pending were Manuel Rojas and Rodulfo Echevarría, as they became subjects of the ongoing dispute between the military and the civil court.[60]

Undaunted, Governor Pavía asked for complete briefs of the five whose sentences he had commuted and ordered their transfer to San Juan. They were to be held in the prison of the Morro Castle until they could be shipped off to Spain. Finally, on 16 December they were put aboard the ship *Santander*, which after a brief stop in Cuba would take them to Spain.[61] He also sent along with the ship's captain a copy of a letter he had supposedly received from the departing prisoners and his own explanation for having commuted their death sentences.

The letter from the rebels, which also appeared in the *Gaceta* on 12 December, thanked Pavía for his clemency, wished him a long, healthy life, and requested permission to see their families before sailing for Spain. They appeared to have repented as they blamed their past revolutionary actions on the poor advice of others.[62]

His reasons for commuting their death sentences, he said, were based on the many pleas for mercy he received from the clergy and dozens of ladies from all over the island. Their claim that the death penalty was too stiff a sentence for first offenders, together with his conviction that the island was no longer in danger, had led him to reduce their punishment to ten years imprisonment.[63] He reminded the Madrid government that on 13 November they had cautioned him not to apply excessive punishment.[64]

By shipping the rebel leaders out of the country, Governor Pavía ended the military proceedings against one sector of the Lares' rebels. But those under Judge Navascués custody continued to be held without having been sentenced. Day after day dozens of prisoners were interrogated, and either sent back to their cells or paroled without any comment as to their guilt or innocence in connection with the uprising.

According to the lists we compiled, a total of 551 persons were charged by the authorities for their alleged participation in the conspiracy and/or attack against Lares and Pepino. Of those, the majority, 523, were seized by the military and put in prison. Only 20 of those charged escaped capture and

106 *Puerto Rico's Revolt for Independence*

TABLE X
Fate of the suspects charged for participating in the conspiracy, the attacks on Lares and Pepino

All	551	(100.0)
Arrested and Jailed	523	(94.9)
Escaped	20	(3.6)
Died from Military Inflicted Wounds	8	(1.5)

Sources: The sources for this table are scattered in the dozens of boxes we consulted. One helpful set of documents contains the lists sent by Judge Navascués to Audiencia on 19 February 1868, which appear in AGPR, FGEPR, *La Revolución de Lares 1868*, Caja 181, Pieza 48.

eight died in the field or in jail as a result of wounds inflicted by the military troops.

On 17 December, Governor Pavía requested a full report of the proceedings against the rebels under Judge Navascués jurisdiction.[65] But the judge explained there was not enough time to do a detailed report and sent him instead several copies of testimonies given by the major rebel leaders and a brief summary of the findings until that moment.[66]

Pavía was removed from office in December of 1868 and by January 1869 the proceedings had been halted by the new Governor, José Laureano Sanz. He ended the entire affair by granting general amnesty.[67] Spain, then involved in a "pacification" war against Cuba, could not afford to let the situation in Puerto Rico go unresolved any longer. Mounting complaints from the coffee region reflected the landowners fears that their coffee crop would be lost if the prisoners were not released soon.[68] There were also rumors that relatives of the prisoners were going to free them by storming the jails.[69] These, added to the Governor's desire to restore the society to normalcy, convinced Sanz to grant general amnesty for all except Rojas and Echevarria whose death sentences he commuted.

Like Pavía, Sanz explained to the Overseas Minister that he spared the lives of those condemned to death because he saw no reason to spill blood after so much time had passed. He added that his decision to grant amnesty to all political prisoners stemmed from his conviction that, in the long run, "such a generous action would prove useful in helping to maintain law and order and to avoid future political complications."[70]

The amnesty decree forwarded by the Governor to Audiencia on 26 January stated that all those politically implicated (in the Lares-Pepino attack) were to be released immediately and all proceedings against them to be terminated.[71]

Five days before Governor Sanz made known his decree, the provisional government in Madrid had reached a similar decision to free the political prisoners of Puerto Rico. But the Madrid decree, which did not reach the Governor's desk until weeks after he had proclaimed his own, was much less generous than the one adopted by Governor Sanz. Essentially, the Madrid decree only granted amnesty to "Spaniards, whether born in Spain or in Puerto Rico." It did not stipulate what was to be done with the foreign political prisoners, such as Rojas and Pedro S. García, who were born in Venezuela and Santo Domingo. Nor did the decree specify whether all the political prisoners sentenced, and pending sentences, were to be freed alike.[72]

At the time Governor Sanz' amnesty was put into effect the investigations conducted by Judge Navascués were not yet completed. As Navascués himself reported several days later, nearly all of the 523 persons arrested were still pending sentence. The exceptions were 5 prisoners Navascués released because they were found to be innocent. Thus the news of Governor Sanz' amnesty was a welcomed relief from the never-ending proceedings of Judge Navascués' court.

Based on Navascués' own reports, at the time amnesty was granted he had paroled 126 persons (see Table XI), released 5 who were innocent, and failed to interrogate 37. Of the remaining, 80 had perished in jail, and 263 were still behind bars.

By 26 January the civil court had interrogated over 90 percent of the 511 prisoners in its custody. According to the comments Navascués included, next to the names of the prisoners he listed for Audiencia, the majority, or 56 percent denied every charge made against them, while the remaining 44 percent confessed to all and/or part of the charges brought against them (see Table XII).

TABLE XI
Status of prisoners under Navascués' custody, January 1869

All	511	(100.0)
Paroled before amnesty was decreed	126	(24.6)
Died in jail	80	(15.6)
Prisoners of unknown status	37	(7.2)
Innocent, released	5	(0.9)
In jail, pending sentences	263	(51.5)

Source: The primary source for this table was a report Judge Navascués submitted to Audiencia on 26 January 1869, in AGPR, FGEPR, *La Revolución de Lares 1868*, Caja 181, Pieza 48.

TABLE XII
Results of the prisoners' interrogations

All	469	(100.0)
Denied all charges	262	(56.0)
Confessed to all charges	185	(39.4)
Confessed to the minor charges	22	(4.6)

Sources: Statistics were compiled by the researcher from various sources, but the most useful sources were the lists provided by Judge Navascués to Audiencia, 19 February 1868, in AGPR, FGEPR, *La Revolución de Lares 1868*, Caja 181, Piezas 47, 48.

Whether the majority of those jailed were innocent or guilty as charged is hard to say since the interrogation did not follow the same line of questioning after mid-October. The purpose and nature of the investigation changed after the Auditor of War ordered Judge Navascués to focus on determining who had taken part in the attack against Pepino. The shift in emphasis, from Navascues' broader goal, which was to uncover the origin, nature, and extent of the conspiracy to the narrower military's quest made it possible for the majority of the prisoners to deny the charges brought against them.

News of the death sentences handed down by the War Council to the rebel leaders who took part in the attack against Pepino spread quickly among the prisoners. From then on they did what they could to avoid being connected with that event.[73] Those who were unable to deny their involvement in the conspiracy and/or in the attack against Lares, confessed to these, but emphatically denied having been anywhere near Pepino.[74] Thus, it is not surprising that while 35 to 40 armed men attacked the plaza of Pepino only seven were eventually convicted for that offense by the War Council.

Finally, the Navascués' report indicates that, of the 469 rebels interrogated, nearly 60 percent had been kept in Aguadilla and 38 percent in Arecibo. Of those, 68 prisoners died of yellow fever in Aguadilla and 11 in Arecibo. Similarly, almost twice as many prisoners had to be paroled in Aguadilla than in Arecibo for fear that they would fall prey to the yellow fever epidemic.[75]

In sum, the legal proceedings against the rebels of Lares lasted four months before they were officially terminated. Those suspected as well as those convicted of taking arms against the government were declared free. Both the local authorities and the metropolitan government had found it wise to forgive them. The five serving their prison sentences in Cadiz (Spain) were promptly released and returned home. In February the Overseas Minister instructed the Governor of Cadiz to release "at once" the rebels Clodomiro

E. Abril, Pedro S. García, Ignacio Balbino Ostolaza, Andrés Pol, and Leoncio Rivera. He was further instructed that should these men want to return to Puerto Rico they were to be sent "at the expense of the state."[76]

While granting general amnesty was undoubtedly a generous act, its motive was more political than humanitarian. As Governor Sanz stated, such a generous act would not only insure returning the society to law and order, but would insure against future political complications. It should be added that the metropolitan government granting such amnesty was itself a provisional government, created by the revolution of 17 September 1868, whose strength was being tested by the uprisings of Puerto Rico and Cuba. Fearing its own instability, the Madrid government could not afford to dissipate its war resources by provoking both islands into war at once. Instead, it chose to seek the cooperation of Puerto Rico in its war against Cuba. Unfortunately, for the 80 who perished in the jails the amnesty decree came much too late.

NOTES

1 *Oficio* del Gobernador Pavía al Teniente coronel de Estado Mayor, Sabino Gamir y Maladeñ, San Juan, 24 September 1868, reprinted in Pérez Moris, *Historia de la Insurrección de Lares*, pp. 177-78.

2 Pérez Moris, Ibid.

3 Pérez Moris, Ibid., p. 179.

4 While Governor Pavía never referred to Gamir's Plan by its name, it was the plan designed by the colonel in 1866 which Pavía put into effect.

5 Pérez Moris, *Historia de la Insurrección de Lares*, p. 180.

6 Copies of the letter and circular sent the military commanders and the regent of Audiencia can be found in AGPR, *Audiencia Territorial*, Tribunal Pleno, Caja 7, Pieza I.

7 Pérez Moris, *Historia de la Insurrección de Lares*, p. 179.

8 Ibid.

9 The list sent by Captain José Pujol, signed in barrio Palomar (Camuy) on 24 September 1868, contained the names of the major members of the Lanzador del Norte society. The document appears in AGPR, FGEPR, *La Revolución de Lares 1868*, Caja 178, Pieza 13.

10 Evidence of this is found in his testimonies given in Arecibo, 24 and 25 September 1868, which appear in AGPR, FGEPR, *La Revolución de Lares 1868*, Caja 178, Pieza 13.

11 The gunpowder and dynamite sticks were unearthed by Sergeant Huelva's men the afternoon of the 25th, according to the report sent by that official to Colonel Iturriaga. For details, see in AGPR, FGEPR, *La Revolución de Lares 1868*, Caja 178, Pieza 13.

12 *Parte* del Coronel Ibarreta al Gobernador Pavía, Puerto Rico, 19 November 1868, in AGPR, FGEPR, *La Revolución de Lares 1868*, Caja 178, Pieza 12 (hereafter as *Parte*, Ibarreta to Pavía, 19 November 1868).

13   *Oficio* del Gobernador Pavía al Coronel J. Manuel de Ibarreta, 30 September 1868, reprinted in Pérez Moris, *Historia de la Insurrección de Lares*, pp. 181-182.

14   Pérez Moris, Ibid.

15   Pérez Moris, Ibid., pp. 183-184.

16   *Parte* del Coronel Francisco Martínez al Comandante de Operaciones, Manuel de Ibarreta, Rio Prieto, 1 October 1868, reprinted in Pérez Moris, *Historia de la Insurrección de Lares*, pp. 184-187 (hereafter as *Parte*, Martínez to Ibarreta, 1 October 1868).

17   *Parte*, Martínez to Ibarreta, 1 October 1868.

18   Bernardo Navarro was a member of the rebel cell Capá Prieto. For details on the charges against Navarro, see in AGPR, FGEPR, *La Revolución de Lares 1868*, Caja 181, Piezas 47, 48.

19   *Parte*, Martínez to Ibarreta, 1 October 1868.

20   The three men captured by Costa in Quiñones' house were: Agustín Lara, Brugman's son-in-law, a black man from Mayagüez, named Andrés Rause, whose crime was to be outside his jurisdiction without the appropriate papers and a jornalero from San Germán, named Silvestre Feliciano. Feliciano and Lara were charged with taking part in the Lares revolt. See in AGPR, FGEPR, "Estado Demostrativo de los Procesados . . . ," Caja 181, Piezas 47, 48.

21   *Parte*, Martínez to Ibarreta, 1 October 1868.

22   *Parte*, Martínez to Ibarreta, 1 October 1868.

23   *Parte*, Martínez to Ibarreta, 1 October 1868.

24   Toledo, according to José Marcial Quiñones, was assassinated in his bed by order of Colonel Martínez. See his account in *Un Poco de Historia Colonial, 1850-1890* (San Juan: Instituto de Cultura Puertorriqueña, 1978), p. 99.

25   *Parte*, Ibarreta to Pavía, 19 November 1868.

26   *Parte* del coronel Martínez al gobernador Pavía, 6 October 1868, in Pérez Moris, *Historia de la Insurrección de Lares*, pp. 190-92. (hereafter as *Parte*, Martínez to Pavía, 6 October 1868).

27   José Marcial Quiñones, *Un Poco de Historia Colonial*, p. 99.

28   Letter from Governor Pavía to Colonel Martínez, 7 October 1868, reprinted in Pérez Moris, *Historia de la Insurrección de Lares*, p. 192.

29   "A los Habitantes de Puerto Rico," San Juan, 8 October 1868, in AGPR, *Audiencia Territorial, Tribunal Pleno*, Caja 7, pp. 51-52.

30   In AGPR, FGEPR, *La Revolución de Lares 1868*, Caja 176, Piezas 2, 3.

31   Many taxpayers offered their support to the military troops in their areas. They volunteered to pay half of their taxes in advance.

32   Copy of Berriz' circular, dated 6 October 1868, was sent by Demetrio Santaella with an explanatory letter. Both documents are found in AGPR, FGEPR, *La Revolución de Lares 1868*, Caja 176, Pieza 3.

33   "Oficio del Gobernador de Puerto Rico comunicando la captura de todos, incluso Rojas . . . ," in Biblioteca Nacional, Madrid, Sección: *Ultramar*, Serie: *Puerto Rico, Poder Ejecutivo*, Vol. I, Expediente 8, Documento 1.

34   *Parte* del Capitán Prats al Gobernador Pavía, 18 October 1868, published in *La Gaceta*, 24 October 1868.

35   Letter from Navascués to Audiencia, 18 October 1868, in AGPR, *Audiencia Territorial, Tribunal Pleno*, Caja 7, Pieza I.

36   Letter from Governor Pavía to the Regent, Puerto Rico, 22 October 1868, in AGPR, *Audiencia Territorial, Tribunal Pleno*, Caja 7, Pieza I.

37 Pavía's "Circular a los Comandantes de Operaciones de Puerto Rico," 18 October 1868, in Pérez Moris, *Historia de la Insurrección de Lares*, p. 197.

38 Copy of the circular, dated 24 October 1868, appears in Pérez Moris, *Historia de la Insurrección de Lares*, pp. 198-200.

39 From Saint Thomas, Puerto Rico continued to receive proclamations. During the months of November and December there were rumors that some towns were planning to revolt, to free the rebels. See letters from the municipalities: Peñuelas, 5 November 1868; Guayama, 13 November 1868; Patillas, 17 November 1868; Manatí, 22 November 1868, in AGPR, FGEPR, *La Revolución de Lares 1868*, Caja 177, Pieza 5.

40 Reported to the Regent of Audiencia by Governor Pavía in his letter of 14 October 1868, in AGPR, *Audiencia Territorial, Tribunal Pleno*, Caja 7, Pieza 1, pp. 56-59.

41 Governor Pavía to Audiencia, 28 September 1868, in *Tribunal Pleno*, Caja 7, Pieza 1.

42 Pavía to the Regent of Audiencia, 29 September 1868, in *Tribunal Pleno*, Caja 7, Pieza 1.

43 "Circular from Audiencia to the judges," 29 September 1868, in AGPR, FGEPR, *La Revolución de Lares 1868*, Caja 176, Pieza 2, p. 96.

46 Navascués' report to Audiencia, from Arecibo, 4 October 1868, in *Audiencia*, Caja 7, Pieza 1, pp. 43-44.

47 Navascués' report to Audiencia from aboard the ship *Aguila*, Aguadilla, 3 October 1868, in *Audiencia*, Caja 7, Pieza 1, pp. 34-35.

48 Ibid.

49 Navascués to Audiencia, Arecibo, 4 October 1868, in *Audiencia*, Caja 7, Pieza 1, pp. 43-44.

50 Navascués to Audiencia, Arecibo, 5 October 1868, in *Audiencia*, Caja 7, Pieza 1, p. 47.

51 Navascués to Audiencia, Lares, 8 October 1868, in *Audiencia*, Caja 7, Pieza 1, pp. 54-55.

52 The list of names given by Ibarra is too long to include it here. However the names of the members of the alleged San Juan society are too important to be omitted. Based on Ibarra's testimony, Navascués ordered the arrest of Julián Eusebio Blanco, José Julián Acosta, Rufino Goenaga, Gerónimo Goico and Calixto Romero, for their cooperation in the conspiracy. Information about the names given by Ibarra appears throughout the investigation, as suspects were brought to testify. The specific names and actions regarding the men from San Juan appear in a communique sent by Audiencia to the district judge of the capital, 16 October 1868, in *Audiencia*, Caja 7, Pieza 1, pp. 55-56.

53 Navascués to Audiencia, Arecibo, 18 October 1868, in *Audiencia*, Caja 7, Pieza 1, p. 68.

54 Pavía to Navascués, 22 October 1868, in *Audiencia*, Caja 7, Pieza I, p. 70.

55 Letter from the Auditor of War to Governor Pavía, 14 October 1868, a copy of which was sent by the Governor to the Regent of Audiencia, 15 October 1868, in *Audiencia*, Caja 7, Pieza 1, pp. 56-59.

56 Letter from Pavía to the Auditor of War, 4 November 1868, in *Audiencia*, Caja 7, Pieza 1, p. 72.

57 Letter from Governor Pavía to the Regent of Audiencia, 4 November 1868, in *Audiencia*, Caja 7, Pieza 1, p. 75.

58 *Parte* del Consejo de Guerra enviada al Gobernador Pavía, 17 November 1868, in Pérez Moris, *Historia de la Insurrección de Lares*, p. 216.

59   *Dictamen* del Gobernador Pavía, Capitanía General de Puerto Rico, 21 November 1868, in Pérez Moris, Ibid.

60   *Oficio* del Gobernador Superior Civil de Puerto Rico al Ministro de Ultramar, 30 November 1868, in Bib. Nac., Madrid, Asuntos: *Puerto Rico*: "Sucesos de Lares," Legajo 20128, Doc. 19.

61   Carta Oficial del Gobernador Superior Civil de Puerto Rico al Ministro de Ultramar, 16 December 1868, Bib. Nac. Madrid, "Sucesos de Lares," Legajo 20128, Doc. 14.

62   A copy of the letter published in *La Gaceta*, 12 December 1868, was reprinted by Pérez Moris, in *Historia de la Insurrección de Lares*, p. 218.

63   *Oficio* del Gobernador Superior Civil al Ministro de Ultramar, 13 December 1868, in Bib. Nac. Madrid, "Sucesos de Lares," Legajo 20128, Doc. 19.

64   *Orden* del Poder Ejecutivo, Ministerio de Ultramar, 13 December 1868, in Bib. Nac. Madrid, Ibid., "Sucesos de Lares," Legajo 20128, Doc. 12.

65   The Governor's request appears in *Boletín de Historia Puertorriqueña*, Vol. II, No. 5 (Abril 1950), p. 152.

66   A detailed description of the documents forwarded by Navascués to the Governor, in lieu of the full report requested, appear in AGPR, FGEPR, *La Revolución de Lares 1868*, Caja 181.

67   See Letter from Governor José Laureano Sanz to the Overseas Minister in Madrid, in Bib. Nac. Madrid, Asuntos: *Puerto Rico*: "Sucesos de Lares," Legajo 20128, Doc. 23.

68   For the need for workers in the coffee region, see Jacinto García Pérez' report to the Governor on 7 November 1868, in AGPR, FGEPR, *La Revolución de Lares 1868*, Caja 177, Pieza 5.

69   In November the Governor received reports, from six mayors of six municipalities, claiming that revolts were being planned, which threatened to include the slaves. Letters in AGPR, FGEPR, *La Revolución de Lares 1868*, Ibid.

70   Carta de José Laureano Sanz al Ministro de Ultramar, Adelardo de Ayala, 10 January 1869, Bib. Nac. Madrid, "Sucesos de Lares," Legajo 20128.

71   Copy of the decree is found in AGPR, *Audiencia*, Caja 7, Pieza 1, p. 100. Also published in *La Gaceta*, 26 January 1869.

72   Carta del Ministerio de Ultramar al Gobernador Superior Civil de Puerto Rico, 28 January 1869, in AGPR, *Obras Públicas, Asuntos Varios*, Caja 144, Legajo 181, Expediente 25.

73   Asked by the judge whether they had gone to Pepino the morning of the 24th, many answered that they had reached the outskirts of the town, but had not entered because they heard the troops were there. Others said that they deserted the rebels on the way to Pepino because they did not want to become involved. Still others, among whom were some leaders from Lares and Mayagüez, stated that they had not entered the plaza because of some problem with their horses.

74   Many of those who confessed to the charge of attacking Lares did so after the judge presented them with concrete evidence linking them to the attack.

75   Statement made by Judge Navascués in his report to *Audiencia*, on 19 February 1869, in AGPR, FGEPR, *La Revolución de Lares 1868*, Caja 181, Pieza 48.

76   Carta del Ministerio de Ultramar al Gobernador de Cadiz, 3 February 1869, in AGPR, *Obras Públicas, Asuntos Varios*, Caja 144, Legajo 181, Exp. 294.

Conclusion

By adopting the premise that provocation occurs not when the metropolis is inert but when it is active, we have demonstrated that El Grito de Lares, like the cries for independence in Spanish America 50 years earlier, was the reaction of a group of colonists against too much metropolitan control.

By comparing the island with other Spanish American colonies it was possible to explain why Puerto Rico's insurrectionary spirit did not develop until the late 1860s. In Puerto Rico, the classical colonization undergone by the Spanish American colonies centuries earlier was just beginning at the end of the eighteenth century, while in Spanish America it was coming to an end. Consequently, the imperial policy Spain adopted during the late eighteenth century could not have had the same effect in the two places. In Spanish America, the new imperial policy helped to accelerate the ongoing process of alienation, culminating in the wars for independence, while in Puerto Rico the same policy served to insure Spain's control over the island. The three centuries of neglect to which the island had been subjected had not made it possible for the colony to produce either the wealth or the powerful creoles that would lead to antagonisms and clashes with Spain as early as 1810.

With the outbreak of war in Spanish America, Puerto Rico became increasingly more important to Spain, as it could be used once again as a military base of operations as well as a "showcase" for Spanish goodwill and reforms. With the loss of Spanish America during the 1820s, Spain became increasingly more dependent on its remaining colonies in the New World. As such, it became more determined to keep those colonies under its control.

To that end, the Crown applied some variations in the colonial policy that alternated between liberal offerings and strict controls. During the war years in Spanish America, Spain found it expedient to shower Puerto Rico with reforms. Trade concessions and tax incentives, for example, helped to generate an economic prosperity which attracted thousands of immigrants from Europe and the New World and inspired great hopes among the creoles. The newcomers added to the population, contributed to the island's production, and helped shape a wealthy class of landowners and merchants which became not only dependent on the colonial government, but loyal to Spain.

113

By the late 1830s, however, Spain, having lost the Spanish Main, was too beset by domestic problems to continue to offer reforms. Thus, it tried to hold on to the colony by resorting to force. The colonial administration was left to the military governors, who with their unlimited powers were expected to prevent colonial problems. Need of resources from the colony and fear of reaction from the top often led Spain to favor the colonial elite at the expense of the laboring classes. As economic prosperity began to vanish, the laboring classes were coerced into subsidizing the development of the economy.

With the expansion of the population, particularly with the penetration of the interior by new immigrants after the mid-1840s, demands for land, trade outlets, and jobs increased, creating new problems the colonial government could not solve. The competition created by the newcomers increasingly became a sore issue between the creoles and the administration. They complained that the newcomers with more resources and/or connections in the administration were better able to compete for the jobs, commercial outlets, and land. Without capital, and deprived of banking and credit facilities, the creoles often became easy prey for the usurious terms the recently arrived merchants imposed.

For the professionals, too, the newcomers came to represent a challenge, as they were generally hired over the creoles in the few jobs available in the administration. Thus, by the 1860s, the demand for jobs was just another issue between the creoles and the Spanish government.

Spain's inability to resolve any of these antagonisms favorably for the dissatisfied creoles led to the conviction among a sector of the intellectuals that the island would be better off without Spain. Thus, they began issuing proclamations in which they argued that Spain not only exploited the island, but had become increasingly tyrannical in recent years. They claimed that Spain was no longer a just parent, for it favored outsiders and peninsulares over them. The more convinced they became that Spain was incapable or unwilling to redress the colonial injustices, the more determined they became of the necessity to break with Spain.

Once the idea of separation from Spain had gained some followers, the separatist leaders tried to enlist others by justifying the break with Spain with political and cultural arguments. For example, they emphasized the need as well as the inevitability of breaking with Spain. Puerto Rico, they said, deserved to be free, for it was not only a separate geographic entity, but a social, cultural, and historical entity as well. Separation, they argued, had happened so naturally over the past years that the only thing lacking to be complete was political independence. And the right to be free, besides being a God-given right, was one they had also earned by years of work and suffering under the unjust rule of Spain.

But oppressive conditions, political ideology, and intellectual revolutionary determination were not enough to liberate the island from the Spanish yoke. Traditionally, the rebels' failure to liberate the island has been attributed to the obvious factors that the revolt began before it was planned, that Betances was kept from coming to their aid, and that the mountains of the island were not big enough to offer much cover for guerrilla warfare. These explanations are only partially valid in our view.

This study demonstrates that the primary reasons for the aborted revolution are found in the colonization process itself. The new colonization that began in the late eighteenth century was still an ongoing process in the 1860s. With the new migratory waves constantly arriving on the island, old groups were increasingly displaced. The state of constant social flux did not allow potentially powerful creole groups to consolidate their power and wealth, as their much stronger counterparts had done in Spanish America during the years of imperial neglect. The onslaught of the new colonization did not allow the time, the resources, nor the opportunity for a creole elite to emerge strong enough to oust Spain.

The rebels also failed because their impoverished condition made it difficult for them to enlist the social support they needed to face up to Spain. Without economic resources and devoid of political power, they could neither purchase the war materiel they needed nor finance the creation of a rebel army. For these ventures they needed the support of at least a sector of the wealthier classes. But in Puerto Rico, getting that support was difficult because the wealthy were generally Spaniards and foreign immigrants loyal to Spain. Even those hacendados who might have cooperated with a revolutionary movement against Spain were deterred by the rebels' program which called for the abolition of slavery and the libreta system. Not one wealthy hacendado joined the rebel cause. Yet many of them put their lives and haciendas at the disposal of the government once the revolt broke out. Dependent as they were on the survival of the coerced labor system, the hacendados thought it safest to side with the colonial system.

Although several hundred jornaleros, slaves and poor persons fought in Lares, the rebel leaders were not very successful in attracting the poorer classes to their cause. The reasons for this problem appear to be twofold: they offered little beyond the promise of liberation to the enslaved and quasi-enslaved population and they made no commitments that once in power they would not resort to the same coercive methods used by Spain. The fact that many of the slaves and jornaleros worked for the men leading the revolt undoubtedly influenced them not to join their cause. In most cases, the poorer classes chose to wait until they were conscripted by force.

Those who joined voluntarily quickly abandoned the rebel ranks when the armed struggle did not give evidence of being able to survive. The leaders lack of military training or experience in the martial arts contributed greatly to their defeat. Their inability to sustain the armed struggle also diminished their chances of securing help from abroad. Not even the determined Betances was able to reach them.

The untimely discovery of their plot, the seasoned troops who had just returned from a war against Santo Domingo, and the counter insurgency measures taken by the Gamir Plan were also important in dooming the rebels' plan.

Yet despite their failure to liberate the island, the rebels made their mark on the island's history and a great impact on Spain. Although on the surface Spain appeared disdainful of the seriousness of the revolt, the post insurrectionary concessions it granted indicates that it was concerned.

After more than 30 years of unfulfilled promises, Spain found it possible to extend to Puerto Rico many of the liberal reforms it was considering for the provinces of the Peninsula. In 1869, Spain extended to the island part of its liberal constitution, as it had done during the years that Spanish America was at war. The colony was awarded provincial status and Spanish citizenship was again granted to the creoles. Political reforms were undertaken, allowing the islanders not only to participate in special elections, but to organize themselves, for the first time, into officially recognized political parties. The abolition of slavery, begun piecemeal in 1869, was finally culminated in 1873. That same year the libreta system was also cancelled.

Although many of these concessions were later sabotaged and some even temporarily cancelled, the fact that they were granted by Spain so soon after the uprising erupted makes one suspect that the efforts of the rebels were not all in vain.

But even if there had been no material gains, El Grito de Lares is still important because it signaled the beginning of a liberation struggle that has yet to be completed. By their actions the rebels of Lares gave Puerto Rico an heroic deed with its own patriotic figures around which future generations could weave revolutionary myths. With the myths, the advocates of independence created new symbols that helped to keep alive the newborn nationalism. Their works, in turn, helped to immortalize the heroic deed as well as nourished the belief that El Grito de Lares gave birth to the Puerto Rican nation.

Bibliography

Bibliographical Aids

de la Peña Marazuela, María Teresa. *Inventario de la Serie de Gobierno de Puerto Rico* (Archivo Histórico Nacional, Madrid: 1972).

Gómez, Canedo, Lino. *Los archivos históricos de Puerto Rico* (San Juan: Instituto de Cultura Puertorriqueña, 1964).

Staff of the Archivo General de Puerto Rico. "Inventario Preliminar del Fondo Municipal de Lares" (Copy facilitated by Laird W. Bergad).

Ulibarri, George S. The National Archives. "Preliminary Inventory of the Records of the Spanish Governos of Puerto Rico" (Record Group 186) Washington, D.C.: 1964).

Primary Sources: Manuscripts

Archivo General de Puerto Rico, San Juan

    Audiencia Territorial, Tribunal Pleno, Caja 7, Pieza 1.

    Colección Emiliano Pol (Lares 1864-1871) "Diario de la casa Marquez, No. 4"; "Diario de la casa Mercantil Amador Fronteras, No. 1."

    Disputación Provincial, Administración Municipal, Lares (1849-1873). Caja 1, Cartapacio 58-A-1.

    Municipalidades, Protocolos Notariales:

Aguadilla	(1851)	Caja 1,284 folios 315-316,
	(1852)	Caja 1,285 folios 125-126,
	(1866)	Caja 1,239 folios 139,
	(1868)	Caja 1,333 folios 191-199.
Camuy	(1866-69)	Caja 1702 folios 54, 75, 187-88, 294, 295, 301.
Lares-	(1844-46)	Caja 1,430 folios 24-25
Aguadilla	(1866-67)	Caja 1,424 folios 39, 54, 82, 153, 163, 180, 230, 325
	(1868)	Caja 1,426 folios 191, 222, 329, 331, 407
	(1869)	Caja 1,427 folios 59, 357, 397, 468.

San   (1862) Caja 1,466 folios 557, 605
Sebastián (1865) Caja 1,469 folios 429, 565
              (1866-67) Caja 1,470 folios 9, 216, 225
              (1868) Caja 1,471 folios 15, 125
              (1869) Caja 1,472 folios 279-80
              (1870) Caja 1,472 folios 107, 144, 224.
Obras Públicas (Asuntos Varios), Caja 144, Legajo 181, Expedientes 25, 294.
Propiedad Pública, Camuy
    (1827-1890) Caja 28.
    Lajas y Lares (1854-1899) Caja 95.
    Lares, Caja 96.
    San Sebastián (1824-1905) Caja 217.
Fondo de los Gobernadores Españoles de Puerto Rico, Asuntos Políticos y Civiles *La Revolución de Lares 1868*,
    Cajas: 176-181; Piezas: 1, 2, 3, 5, 10, 11, 12, 13, 38, 39, 40, 41, 42, 43, 44, 46, 47, 48. Also the *Informe Final* del Juez Don Nicasio de Navascués y Aisa, 19 de febrero de 1869, in *La Revolución de Lares 1868*, Caja 181, Pieza 48.
    Municipalities (Lares 1830-50) Caja 485, Entry 273. Also (Lares, 1860-1890) Caja 486, Folder No. 1860.
Tribunal Superior, Mayagüez, Causas Civiles, Caja 2, Legajo 51.
Archivo Histórico Nacional, Madrid
    Gobierno de Puerto Rico, Legajo 5,088, Expedientes 1-3.
    Gobierno, Legajo 5,110, Expedientes 23-32, 34, 35, (These documents appeared in the old listings of the Biblioteca Nacional, Madrid as Legajo 20128, (Expediente No. 60) (68 Documentos). We also consulted several microfilm copies of documents related to *La Insurrección de Lares*, Legajo 5,111, Expendiente 34 (Carrete 7 Microfilm) at the *Centro de Investigaciones Históricas*, Universidad de Puerto Rico.
Archivo Municipal de Mayagüez
    (Documentos Municipales) (Bound Documents) Volumes I, II (1866), Volume II (1867), Volume I (1869).
Archivo Nacional de Cuba
    (Copies at the *Centro de Investigaciones Históricas*, Universidad de Puerto Rico).
    Asuntos Políticos, Legajo 55, signatura 15, oficio 99 15 fs.
    Intendencia, Legajo 829, Expediente No. 4 (13 fs).
Biblioteca Nacional, Madrid
    Ultramar, Puerto Rico, Poder Ejecutivo, Vol. I, Expediente 8, Doc. 1.
The National Archives, Washington, D.C.
    State Department Consular Despatches, San Juan, Puerto Rico, Volume II, 1867-68, Despatches 22, 39, 55, 79, 90, 91, 104.

Primary Sources: Printed Documents and Contemporary Accounts

Abbad y Lasierra, Fray Iñigo. *Historia Geográfica Civil y Natural de la Isla de San Juan de Puerto Rico*, new edition annotated by José Julián Acosta y Calbo (Puerto Rico: 1866).

Bonafoux, Luis. *Betances*, 2nd Edition, (San Juan: Instituto de Cultura Puertorriqueña, 1970).

Brugman, Arturo. Interview with Arturo Brugman. *La Correspondencia* (New York City) 28 February 1941, pp. 4, 24.

Carroll, Henry K. *Report on Porto Rico, with recommendations, 1899* (Treasury Department Doc. 2118) (Washington, D.C.: Government Printing Office, 1900).

"Carta del Consul Americano en San Juan informando a su gobierno lo ocurrido en Lares, *Historia*, Vol. 2, (Abril-Octubre 1952).

Coll y Toste, Cayetano. *Boletín Histórico de Puerto Rico*, 14 Vols. (San Juan: Tip. Cantero Fernandez, 1914-27).

La Gaceta 2 March 1824.

La Gaceta 26 January 1869.

Morales Muñoz, Generoso. *Boletín de Historia Puertorriqueña*, Vol. II, Nos. 2, 3, 4, 5, 6, 7, (enero-junio 1950).

Ormachea, Darío. "Memoria acerca de la agricultura, el comercio y las rentas interiores de la isla de Puerto Rico (Madrid, 1847), reprinted in Cayetano Coll y Toste, ed., *Boletín Histórico de Puerto Rico*, II.

Pérez Moris José y Luis Cueto. *Historia de la Insurrección de Lares* (Río Piedras: Editorial Edil, 1975). Reprint of the 1872 edition published by Establecimiento Tip. de Narciso Ramírez y Co.

Partido Nacionalista. "Proclamas del Nacionalismo, 1930-1935" (Lares, Puerto Rico: Ediciones Año-Pre-Centenario de la Proclamación de la República, 1967).

Proyecto para la Abolición de la Esclavitud en Puerto Rico (San Juan: Instituto de Cultura Puertorriqueña, 1959).

Puerto Rico, Estadística General del Comercio Exterior de Puerto Rico, 1862-1898, Vol. 27V, In-15 HF-155,A3, Microfilm copy, Shelf 32989 (Photoduplication service, 1971) Library of Congress, Washington, D.C.

Tapia y Rivera, Alejandro. *Mis Memorias ó Puerto Rico como lo Encontré y como lo Dejo* (New York: 1927). Reprint by Editorial Edil, 1971.

The New York Herald. 3 August 1867.

Ubeda y Delgado, Manuel. *Isla de Puerto Rico: Estudio Histórico, Geográfico y Estadístico* (Puerto Rico: Establecimiento Tipográfico del Boletín, 1878).

United States, War Department, *Report of the Census of Porto Rico, 1899* (Washington, D.C.: Government Printing Office, 1900).

Secondary Sources

Andreu Iglesias, Cesar. "El Grito de Lares y la Actualidad Puertorriqueña" (conferencia dictada en las casa de los Trabajadores en San Juan, en conmemoración del Octagésimo aniversario del Grito de Lares, 23 de Septiembre 1948).

Baralt, Guillermo. *Esclavos Rebeldes* (Río Piedras: Ediciones Huracán, 1981).

Bergad, Laird. "Agrarian History of Puerto Rico, 1870-1930," in *Latin American Research Review*, Vol. XIII, No. 3 (1978), pp. 63-94.

____. "Hacia El Grito de Lares: Café, Estratificación Social y Conflictos de Clase 1828-1868," in Francisco A. Scarano, Editor. *Inmigración y Clases Sociales en el Puerto Rico del Siglo XIX* (Río Piedras: Ediciones Huracán, 1981), pp. 183-185.

Blasier, Cole. "Social Revolution: Origins in Mexico Bolivia, and Cuba." In Rolando Bonachea and Nelson Valdés, editors, *Cuba in Revolution* (Garden City, New York: Doubleday and Co. Inc., 1972).

Brau, Salvador. *Historia de Puerto Rico* (New York: D. Appleton and Company, 1904). Reprint by Editorial "El Coquí," 1966.

____. "Las Clases Jornaleras de Puerto Rico." In *Ensayos: Disquisiciones Sociológicas* (Río Piedras: Editorial Edil, 1972).

Brinton, Crane. *The Anatomy of Revolution* (New York: Vintage Books, 1952).

Buitrago Ortiz, Carlos. *Los orígenes históricos de la sociedad precapitalista en Puerto Rico* (Río Piedras, P.R.: Ediciones Huracán Inc., 1976).

Carreras, Carlos N. *Betances: El Antillano Proscrito* (San Juan: Editorial Club de la Prensa, 1961).

Carro Figueroa, Vivian. "La Formación de la gran propiedad cafetalera: La Hacienda Pietri, 1858-1898," *Anales de Investigación Histórica* (Universidad de Puerto Rico, San Juan), Vol. II, No. 1, (Enero-Junio, 1975).

Centro de Investigaciones Históricas. *El Proceso Abolicionista en Puerto Rico: Documentos para su Estudio*. Vol. I (San Juan: Instituto de Cultura Puertorriqueña, 1974).

Cepero-Bonilla, Raul. *Azúcar y Abolición* (Barcelona: Editorial Crítica, S.A., 1976).

Cifre de Loubriel, Estela. *La formación del pueblo puertorriqueño: La contribución de los catalanes, baléaricos, y valencianos* (San Juan: Instituto de Cultura Puertorriqueña, 1975).

Corretjer, Juan Antonio. "The Day Puerto Rico Became a Nation." *The San Juan Star Sunday Magazine*, 22 September 1968.

____. *La Lucha por la Independencia de Puerto Rico*, 4ta Edición (Guaynabo, Puerto Rico: Cooperativa de Artes Gráficas, Romualdo Real, 1974).

Cruz Monclova, Lidio. "The Puerto Rican Political Movement in the 19th Century." In *The United States-Puerto Rico Commission Report on the Status of Puerto Rico* (Washington, D.C.: Government Printing Office, 1966).

___. *Historia de Puerto Rico (Siglo XIX)*, 3 vols. (San Juan: Editorial Universitaria, 1958).

___. "El Grito de Lares." (San Juan: Instituto de Cultura Puertorriqueña, 1968).

Cubano Iguina, Astrid. "La Economía Arecibeña del siglo XIX: Identificación de Productores y comerciantes," *Anales de Investigación Histórica*, Vol. VI, No. 1. (Enero-Junio, 1979).

de Hostos, Adolfo. *Diccionario Histórico Bibliográfico Comentado de Puerto Rico* (San Juan: Instituto de Cultura Puertorriqueña, 1976).

Diaz Soler, Luis. *Historia de la esclavitud negra en Puerto Rico (1493-1890)*. 2nd. Edition (Río Piedras: Editorial Universitaria, Universidad de Puerto Rico, 1965).

Dinwiddie, William. *Puerto Rico: Its Conditions and Possibilities* (New York and London: Harper and Brothers, 1899).

Eckstein, Harry. "On Etiology of Internal War." *History and Theory*, No. 4 (1965).

Enciclopedia de Clásicos de Puerto Rico, 6 Vols. (San Juan: Ediciones Latinoamericanas, 1971), Vol. VI.

Fernández Almagro, Melchor. *Historia Política de la España Contemporanea*, 1868-1885 (Madrid: Alianza Editorial, 1969).

Fernández-Méndez, Eugenio. *Historia Cultural de Puerto Rico 1493-1968* (San Juan: Ediciones "El Cemí," 1970).

Figueroa, Loida. *History of Puerto Rico* (New York: Las Americas Publishing, 1972).

___. *Tres Puntos Claves* (Río Piedras, Puerto Rico: Editorial Edil, 1972).

Figueroa, Sotero. "La Verdad de la Historia," *Patria*, No. 2 (New York), May 1892.

Geigel Polanco, Vicente. "El Grito de Lares: Gesta de Heroismo y Sacrificio." (Rio Piedras: Puerto Rico: 1976).

Gil Bermejo, Juana. *Panorama Histórico de la Agricultura en Puerto Rico* (Sevilla: 1970).

Gómez Acevedo, Labor. *Organización y Reglamentación del Trabajo en el Puerto Rico del Siglo XIX (Propietarios y Jornaleros)* (San Juan: Instituto de Cultura Puertorriqueña, 1970).

Gonzalez, José Luis. *Literatura y Sociedad en Puerto Rico* (Mexico: Fondo de Cultura Económica, 1976).

González Vales, Luis E. *Alejandro Ramírez y su Tiempo* (Río Piedras: Editorial Universitaria, Universidad de Puerto Rico, 1978).

___. "Towards a Plantation Society," in Arturo Morales Carrión, Editor. *Puerto Rico: A Political and Cultural History* (New York: W. W. Norton & Co., Inc., 1983), pp. 79-107.

122 Puerto Rico's Revolt for Independence

Hernández, Pedro J. "Los inmigrantes Italianos de Puerto Rico, durante el siglo XIX," *Anales de Investigación Historica*, Vol. III, No. 2 (1976).

Huberman, Leo and Paul M. Sweezy. *Cuba: The Anatomy of a Revolution* (New York: Monthly Review Press, 1961).

Lynch, John. *The Spanish-American Revolutions, 1808-1826* (New York: W. W. Norton and Company, 1973).

Maldonado Denis, Manuel. *Puerto Rico: A Socio-Historic Interpretation* (New York: Vintage Books, (Random House) 1972).

Mayagüez. *Historia de Mayagüez* (Mayagüez, Puerto Rico: 1966).

Medina Ramírez, Ramón. *El Movimiento Libertador en la Historia de Puerto Rico*, 3 vols. (San Juan: Imprenta Nacional, 1959).

Miller, Paul G. *Historia de Puerto Rico* (New York: Rand McNally, 1939).

Morales Carrión, Arturo. *Puerto Rico and the Non-Hispanic Caribbean* (San Juan: University of Puerto Rico Press, 1971).

Moralez Muñoz, Generoso. *Fundación del Pueblo de Lares* (San Juan: Imprenta Venezuela, 1946).

Ojeda Reyes, Felix. "Diez Meses de Misión Confidencial a Estados Unidos," *Historia y Revolución* (Publicación del Grupo de Investigaciones Históricas del Partido Socialista Puertorriqueño) Año I, No. 1 (Septiembre 1976).

Patch, Richard W. "Bolivia: The Restrained Revolution," *Annals of the Academy of Political and Social Services*, Vol. 334 (1961).

Perloff, Harvey S. *Puerto Rico's Economic Future* (Chicago: University of Chicago Press, 1950).

Picó, Fernando S. J. *Registro General de jornaleros* (Utuado, Puerto Rico, 1849-1850) (Río Piedras, Puerto Rico: Ediciones Huracán, 1976).

_____. *Libertad y Servibumbre en el Puerto Rico de siglo XIX* (Río Piedras: Ediciones Huracán, 1979).

_____. *Amargo Café* (Río Piedras: Ediciones Huracán, 1981).

_____. "Deshumanización del trabajo, cosificación de la naturaleza: los comienzos del café en el Utuado del siglo xix," in Francisco A. Scarano, Editor. *Inmigración y Clases Sociales en el Puerto Rico del Siglo XIX* (Río Piedras: Ediciones Huracán, 1981), pp. 187-206.

Picó, Rafael. *Geografía de Puerto Rico* (Río Piedras: Editorial Universitaria, 1954).

Quiñones, José Marcial. *Un Poco de Historia Colonial* (San Juan: Instituto de Cultura Puertorriqueña, 1978).

Quiñones, Francisco Mariano. *Apuntes para la Historia de Puerto Rico* (Mayagüez, Puerto Rico: Tipografía Comercial, 1888).

Quintero Rivera, Angel. "Background to the Emergence of the Imperialist Capitalism in Puerto Rico." In Adalberto López and James Petras, *Puerto Rico and the Puerto Ricans: Studies in History and Society* (New York: Halsted Press, 1974).

——. "Conflictos de clase en la política colonial: Puerto Rico bajo España y bajo los Estados unidos, 1870-1924." Río Piedras: Centro de Estudios de la Realidad Puertorriqueña, 1974, No. 2. Mimeographed.

Rivera, Antonio. "Ubicación de un Municipio: Lares," *Historia*, Vol. 5, No. 1 (Abril 1955).

Sanchez Tarniella, Andrés. *La Economía de Puerto Rico* (Hato Rey, Puerto Rico: Ediciones Bayoan, 1973).

Scarano, Francisco A. "Inmigración y estructura de clases: los hacendados de Ponce, 1815-1845," in Scarano, *Inmigración y Clases Sociales*, 1981, pp. 21-66.

Suárez Díaz, Ada. *El Doctor Ramón Emeterio Betances: Su Vida y Su Obra* (San Juan: Talleres Gráficos Inter Americanos, 1970).

——. "Segundo Ruiz Belvis (Hormigueros, Puerto Rico, 1829-Valparaíso, Chile, 1867") in *Caribe*, Año 11, No. 4 (1982).

Tió Aurelio, Editor. "La identidad de los restos del patricio Lcdo. Segundo Ruiz Belvis." *Boletín de la Academia Puertorriqueña de la Historia* Vol. III, No. 9 (Enero 1973).

Todd, Roberto H. "La Vida Gloriosa de Ramón Emeterio Betances," (conferencia dictada en el Ateneo Puertorriqueño, en commemoración del aniversario del nacimiento de Betances), also published in *El Mundo*, April 11, 1937, pp. 4, 12.

Torre de Alba, María Luisa. "Testamentos en Lares, 1849-1899," *Anales de Investigación Histórica* Vol. III, No. 2 (1976).

Van Middeldyk, R. A. *The History of Puerto Rico from the Spanish Discovery to the American Occupation* (New York: D. Appleton and Co., Inc. 1903).

Vicuña Mackenna, Benjamín. "La Independencia de Cuba y Puerto Rico," *Revista Cubana* (Publicaciones de la Secretaria de Educación, Dirección de Cultura, Las Habana, Cuba), Vol. III, Nos. 7, 8 (Agosto-Septiembre, 1935), pp. 349-350.

Vizcarrondo, Julio L. *Elementos de Historia y Geografía de la Isla de Puerto Rico* (San Juan: Imprenta Militar de J. González, 1863).

Wagenheim, Kal. *Puerto Rico: A Profile* (New York: Praeger Publishers, 1970).

Zeno-Gandía, Manuel. *La Charca* (San Juan: Instituto de Cultura Puertorriqueña, 1966).

Index

Lares uprising, achievements of: 116; reasons for: 113-116; significance of: xi-xv, 116

Living conditions, eighteenth century: 2; nineteenth century: 9, 13, 17, 19-21; hunger: 20

Mangual, Manuel María: 10, 45

Marchesi, Governor José María, letter from: 59-60

Mayagüez, agriculture of: 44, 45; conspiracy of: 67, 68; economic problems of: 10-11, 45-46; municipal budget of: 44; population of: 44

Méndez, Aurelio: 67-68, 86

Merchants of Lares: 47-49; imprisoned by rebels: 85-86

Millán, Clemente: 67-68, 84, 86, 89, 100

Motives for Lares uprising: 14, 15, 38-52, 63, 113-116

Mutiny of Spanish artillery troops, 1867: 58-59

Navascués y Aisa, Judge Nicasio de: 38, 43, 102-104, 107, 108

Occupations of general population: 22, 33-35, 39; rebels: 33

O'Reilly, Marshal Alejandro: 1-3, 23-24

Ostolaza, Ignacio Balbino: 85, 101, 105, 109

Parrilla, Joaquín: 51, 67, 85, 87, 101, 102

Pavía, Governor Julián Juan: 38, 41, 43, 44, 97, 101-106

Pepino, Battle of: 89-91

Pol, Andrés: 50, 67, 82, 87, 100, 105, 109

Pol, Bernabé: 50-52, 86-87

Political conditions: *see* Spanish colonial administration

Population, eighteenth century: 2, 3; nineteenth century: 16-24; racial composition: 16, 22; social classes: 18, 19, 21

Power y Giralt, Ramón: 4

Ramírez, Intendant Alejandro: 4

Ramírez, Francisco: 43, 49, 67-68, 86, 88-89, 91, 100

Ramírez, Manuel: 49, 50, 67, 70, 101

Rebels, characteristics of: 29-38; ages of: 36, 37; birthplaces of: 29-31; debts to merchants: 48-51; literacy of: 33, 35-36; occupations of: 34-35; residences of: 31-32

Rebels, identities of: 62-63, 66-70, 79-91

Rebels, motives of: *see* Motives for Lares uprising

Rebels as prisoners: 97-109; amnesty: 106, 107; capture: 98-101; deaths in prison: 101, 106-107; death sentences: 105, 108, 109; status of: 107-108

Republic of Puerto Rico proclaimed: 82-92

Revolution aborted: 115-116

Revolutionary cells: 43, 48, 50-51, 64-70, 79-83

Revolutionary proclamations: 38-43

Rojas Luzardo, Manuel: 43, 48, 49, 66-67, 69, 81-82, 84-91, 97, 100-102, 105, 107

Ruiz Belvis, Segundo: 57-59, 62-63

Sanz, Governor José Laureano: 106-107, 109

Spanish colonial administration, eighteenth century: 1, 2; nineteenth

About the Book and the Author

This book examines the social and economic forces that led to Puerto Rico's first armed struggle against the island's colonial rulers. In her interpretations the author, Dr. Olga Jiménez de Wagenheim, places the 1868 rebellion known as "El Grito de Lares" within the context of the imperial policies and the major events taking place on the island.

She addresses as well the reasons why Puerto Rico began its struggle against Spain decades after many of the other Spanish colonies had achieved their independence. Making use of extensive previously unresearched archival material, she examines the social and economic backgrounds of the leaders of the rebel movement, and corrects errors of earlier accounts of the revolt. But above all, she brings out the human qualities of the men involved in the revolt.

In Puerto Rico, where the subject of *El Grito De Lares* has been passionately discussed for many years, the book elicited strong emotional reactions from its readers. The reviewer for *El Nuevo Dia,* for example, commented that "the book has the power to cause deep impact upon the reader. . . . Its fascinating reading makes us witnesses of an episode in our history that was both great and tragic." While a reviewer for *El Mundo* concluded that "this book represents, without doubt, the most complete study of the insurrection of September 23, 1868, which has become to many a symbol of Puerto Rican national identity." Another reviewer for the same journal stated, "The narration of events, of the fusion—and confusion—of boldness and fear, of dexterity and blunder, of plans and fortuitous conditions, produce the true pleasure of reading this book."

Dr. Olga Jiménez de Wagenheim is Associate Professor in the Department of History, at Rutgers, The State University of New Jersey, Newark Campus. She is the recipient of a Fulbright Teaching Fellowship to Argentina, the Rutgers Outstanding Teacher of the Year Award, and the post of Distinguished Visiting Hispanic Scholar at William Paterson College. She is co-editor of *The Puerto Ricans: A Documentary History* (Praeger, 1973) and author of *El Grito de Lares: sus causas y sus hombres* (Huracan, 1984) and *Puerto Rico's Revolt for Independence: El Grito de Lares* (Westviev, 1985).